Par
in My

Parenting
Q & A

vol. 1

To Colin + Ann,

Hope you guys find a
nugget or two in here
+ if not it should make
a decent doorstep !!

Parenting in My Pocket Parenting Q & A vol. 1
Copyright ©2020 Allen O'Donoghue

Transcription by: Julie Stevenson
Book Design by: Maria C. A. Fowler
Photo credits:
"Activities" Photo by Giorgio Trovato / Unsplash
"Grief & Loss" Photo by Ksenia Makagonova / Unsplash
"Being A Parent" Photo by Nicholas Githiri / Pexels

Ebook ISBN: 978-1-8382593-1-0
Paperback ISBN: 978-1-8382593-0-3

www.helpme2parent.ie

Parenting
in My Pocket

Parenting
Q & A
vol. 1

by Allen O'Donoghue

Help Me
To Parent

To Julie, Amie-Mai & April
You mean everything to me.

Table of Contents

About the Q & A Format

Over the years of working with families, I would regularly get questions sent to me via every channel there is. I have always committed to answering every question I get, as I believe that if someone takes the time to email me, it's obviously a big enough issue for them and they deserve a reply. I then started to think about how beneficial these questions and answers might be to others, and so the seeds of the Live Q & A were first sown. In 2018, I decided to take the plunge and start dealing with questions live, and I thoroughly enjoyed the process. From the feedback that's come our way, many parents have found some reassurance knowing that others have experienced similar issues with bringing up their children.

The Parenting In My Pocket weekly video is now carrying on the mantle and is building week-on-week. Thank you to every parent who has sent in questions over the years, this book wouldn't be here without you.

ACTIVITIES

Q. I'm a working mum and my husband works, too, full time. We have 2 small children and feel guilty about not having enough time with them in the evenings. We try to cram in playing, but sometimes it leads to chaos and ends up with upset children and frustrated parents. What can we do as parents to make quality time with our kids, even if it is limited, that doesn't end in over-tired and excited kids?

A. This comes up a lot with parents we work with. We feel as parents that we need to give our kids loads of attention and help them experience as much as possible to give them the best life. If we are working all day and come home with an hour or so left before the children go to bed, we feel we need to fit everything in this time, but this is crazy. Your children are going to experience loads of what life has to offer whether you are there or not, you don't need to feel you have to be there to oversee everything your children experience.

Your kids have gone through the day in school, crèche, or with grandparents, and it's been a busy day and they will be tired. They will be excited to see you, but we all need a wind down time. If, when you come home and start busy load games like chasing each other, or playing active games, and then all of a sudden it's time for bed, your children will have a breakdown and possibly start to cry because the fun time is over and now they have to sleep. It's not fair on anyone to do this; kids cry, and parents become frustrated, but it's something in your control.

A lot of parents complain about how difficult bedtime can be, and, yes, it can be, but if you can, put in place a wind down routine where you are spending lovely, quiet, close time with your child when everyone gets to switch off and calm our minds and bodies before bed. You are still with your child, still catching up on their day, but doing it in a more peaceful manner. Do a jigsaw puzzle or read a story. A bath before bed is a lovely relaxing and calming time for children, too, just keep the play to a minimum.

During the week is very busy, and nowadays the weekends can be just as crazy with sporting activities, parties, family commitments. Come

Sunday evening everyone can be feeling very tired and not getting as much rest as is needed. You need to be ok with having a pyjama day or afternoon at the weekend; sit around and watch a family movie and just ignore what's going on outside for a bit. All parts of the human body need rest and recovery and that includes the brain, too. Take the pressure off yourself and your family.

During the week have the calm down time in the evenings, which will hopefully help everyone relax and have better sleep. They will enjoy this time with you just as much as the crazy fun play.

Ignore the Facebook, Instagram, Twitter posts of family and friends who seem to have done all the perfect family events at the weekend, which you didn't do. Concentrate on your family and what's right for you. Go easy on yourselves and enjoy the quieter times too.

Q. My kids are all involved in soccer and two also play musical instruments. They enjoy these activities and want to be involved in them but have to be nagged at constantly to practice. I know they could improve their skills tremendously if they would only make a little effort. How do I encourage without having to constantly nag and push?

A. This is tough. So, you have children taking part in sports and music and they don't practice enough. Who do they not practice enough for? Is it you or is it them? Parents struggle with the balance between not pushing them to the point of arguments and encouraging them in the correct way. You need to set aside the time for the practice, even if it's only 10 minutes. Children don't need to be practicing for hours unless they want to themselves and you want them to become a professional athlete or musician. Even so, they may do all the practice you want them to do and turn around at 18 and they'll tell you they've had enough! The fact they enjoy the activities is really important. Make the practice realistic, 10 – 20 minutes and get involved too. Listen to them play the music or help them with their sports training. This will show them your interest in what they are doing, but don't make it an unpleasant experience.

If your children are really set on doing well with their activities and are doing this amount of practice but soon realise it's not enough to keep up with team mates, they will realise this themselves and will look to do more practice. Once you've done this and encouraged them as much as you can and they decide that something isn't for them, you can sit down and have that discussion.

Q. My son loves football. I don't just mean he loves football; he adores it. He plays football every day, he goes to school with his football kit under his clothes. He gets home and all he wants to do is go play football. He doesn't want to do his homework; he has no interest in school. How do I help him get the balance between football and doing work and knowing there's more to life than football?

A. What I will say is there is nothing more important than football, and that's it!!! All joking aside, this could be written about me; I did the same, football socks and all. It's alright to put a boundary in place, getting a bit of balance in place. Your son may grow up to be a very successful football player and have all the glory that comes with the profession and his schooling may be something that doesn't develop in the same way and that's great. On the other hand, he may not—it may never happen and that's ok, too. It might just be a hobby all the way through the rest of his life.

It's ok to put a time limit on his football playing and homework needs to be done first so it's out of the way and then the rest of the day is all his to play football. Sometimes this may not work out, maybe sometimes he'll need to just go out when he gets home and kick the football around for a bit. Your son will already have done a full day of learning, having to listen and do what he's been told for several hours. Don't get into an argument about it, if he needs 30 minutes of football before he sits down to do the homework, so be it. It might seem like a pain to do it, but if he is willing, comes in and settles down to do his homework, then it's worked. If he's making a fuss when he must come in and refuses to do his homework, then you'll need to sit down with him and explain that he can't have it every way. You are happy for him to go play football before homework, but he must come in and do it when he is asked otherwise it will be homework first and possibly no football if he doesn't do as he is asked. It's all learning and trying to figure out what works best. With everything that we discuss here, there is always room for change and seeing what works best for your family. Every family is different.

Q. I know it's only April, but every Christmas we are under serious pressure financially. Everyone says to start saving, but we don't have any real spare cash to save, and we usually have to put any saving towards something else. Obviously, we have to change something, but can you think of any simple ways to do this.

A. Christmas can catch a lot of people out or it costs a lot more than we expected. I know here in Drogheda, there are a number of local businesses that run penny banks or Christmas clubs, and you can pop your few euro into them every week. By the time Christmas comes along, you have a pot of money to help with the costs. Make sure you are putting in what you can afford to put in and not leaving yourself short every week for the household essentials. You could open a post office account or special bank account that the money goes into and you won't go near until Christmas.

If you don't have the spare money to put away every week, and you are worried about the cost of Christmas, it might be time to look at your overall weekly or monthly spending and see is there anywhere you can cut back. Perhaps you could look at shopping around for your different insurances or energy providers. Can you shop differently, is there a supermarket that offers better deals. If you smoke or drink can you reduce the amount you spend on these things during the week. It could be a really good incentive to stop smoking especially if you are trying to. It's amazing the savings you can make when you put a bit of time aside and shop around. Doing this alone could give you the extra bit of cash you need to put towards Christmas.

My wife started a new saving ritual this year, she heard on the radio. Starting on the first Monday of the year you put €1 away, then on the second Monday you put €2 in, the third €3 until when you get to the Monday of the 52nd week of the year you put €52 in the pot. By the end of the year you should have over €1,000 saved. If you are able to put the amounts away each week it is a very effective way of saving but you need to make sure you're not dipping into if you need to.

You could try and spread the costs during the year by picking up gifts when sales are on. It's also really important to look at what you are spending the money on at Christmas and see are there places you can reduce the spending on. Nobody wants to have to worry about the cost of Christmas, but, in reality, thousands of people get themselves into massive debt for one day of the year and it's not until January that the true cost comes out and it can be a very stressful way to start the new year.

Q. Myself and my friend have children playing football together. It's great and I love going to watch them play. The issue is that he is constantly shouting at everyone during the match: his son, the coach, the ref, and it's really over the top. It's clear his son is embarrassed, but he seems oblivious. How do I say it to him without it affecting our friendship?

A. That's difficult especially since you have a friendship with this person, and you want to keep it. It's something that a lot of sports clubs are trying to stamp out pitch side as parents are starting to become overly involved in the match and it is affecting how their child plays and the other children on both teams. A number of clubs have specifically asked for silent side lines which is a really good idea. We all want our children to do the best they can but there is a big difference between encouraging them and then coaching them in a negative manner if they don't get the ball or miss a goal. As parents it's very difficult not to jump in, especially if we feel our child or their team is being hard done by. It's really embarrassing for our children to hear us shouting and roaring at other coaches or the ref, they don't need that, and we need to learn to respect that.

Perhaps have a word with the team coach and ask if they have heard the shouting and how do they feel about it. If it's something they are increasingly aware of and are worried about, it may be worth calling a meeting of the parents, even just a quick chat after a game to let the parents know that there is a code of conduct for coaches and parents at the matches, and have a piece of paper ready to get signatures that parents agree to this. That parents must keep their voices and opinions down during the match and allow the players to play, the refs to ref, and the coaches to coach. If there is an issue during the match and the parent is aware of the code of conduct, then they can be asked to stop shouting or, if need be, leave the pitch. Of course, no one wants to see this happen, and hopefully by having the conversation with the parents and getting them to agree to the code of conduct, this behaviour won't happen. There needs to be openness, the coach needs to let parents know that the sideline behaviour of shouting, is not acceptable, and only clapping or positive cheering is encouraged. Maybe your child's coach isn't great, perhaps they are not getting it right, but if that's the case, get involved, too, help out. If your child is happy playing with their friends, then that's all that counts. Coaches move on and children move on to different teams, too, so it's all short term.

If your friend is really over the top and you feel you can say it to them, ask them does their child not get embarrassed by all the shouting they do. Let them know that your child asked you to stop doing it as it put them off and embarrassed them. Your friend might pick up on what you are trying to say, and you'll still have your friendship!

Q. My kids are about to finish school for the summer. We're all really looking forward to the break from the routine, but I'm a bit worried that they'll be bored after the first couple of weeks. Any suggestions?

A. Thousands and thousands of parents across the world are coming up with the same concerns. Summer is a great time for children. Remembering my own, the days were filled with adventures with my friends, nothing really organised. We would head out in the morning and arrive back when we were hungry, and they were brilliant times. It's really important to allow your children to have summers like this too, when we don't try to organise every day for them, because it just won't work.

Children need downtime and need days when they do nothing. Their brains have been working non-stop for whatever amount of months in school, plus their bodies have been going with all the organised after school activities they've been involved in. It's sometimes good for our children to feel bored and to allow their minds and bodies to experience down time and switch off. A number of children I have worked with who suffer from anxiety, have very busy lives and a lot of pressure to be involved in so much, and they are not being given the chance to stop, breathe, and do nothing. So many parents want their children involved in so many activities and excel in school because they want them to achieve and possibly find a sport that they will become professional in or follow a certain successful job path. We, as parents, need to switch our heads off so our children can switch off too.

My own daughter came to me during the holidays to tell me she was bored and I did the usual thing of telling her to find something to do or I will find something for you to do, which won't be as fun as the thing you find to do! She was gone, didn't hear from her again, and there she was doing a fantastic drawing. She found a tutorial online, followed it, and was lost in it. Since then, she has become an avid drawer, and it allows her to lose herself; she completely switches off when she is drawing. She knows it is one of the tools that helps her to relax, switch off, and she is really enjoying it.

Let your children have fun with their friends, be out and about with no real plans, and let them get bored and find new things to do. Of course, this freedom isn't always possible for children if parents have to work and they need a structured activity to do. This is when it may be a really good time to sit down with your children and ask them what it is, they would like to do if they have to go to camps. There could be something new that they have never tried, or something they really love. There could also be friends going on some of these camps, too, which will make it really fun for everyone.

So, mix it up a bit, have the organised camps if needed, as they are a break for everyone, but also try and have the days when there are no plans. There are no alarms going off in the morning, no fixed routine, and see how the day goes. Don't try and feel you need to have them involved and busy all the time; you will all benefit from it in the end. It may take you a few attempts to get used to the more relaxed routine but give it a try.

Q. My husband is a motorbike nut. He's always tinkering with his bike. He now wants to get our 6-year-old daughter into biking. It's fine for him, but I'm really scared she'll get hurt. He's always talking about all the injuries he's had over the years, and I don't want that for her. I know if I get into it with him, it'll cause a huge argument. Have you any advice on how I can talk to him about my concerns?

A. If you feel very really strongly about this, you need to have a conversation with your husband. It may need to come from the perspective of how to keep your daughter safe if she is going to get involved with this pastime with your husband. I'm sure there is no way your husband wants your daughter to get hurt, and her safety is the most important thing. Reframe the situation instead of looking at it as if your daughter is certain to end up with broken limbs or worse. This can be a lovely time for your husband and daughter to bond and get to know each other better. So put a plan in place to keep her safe, and what he is going to do. Don't let him pass over this as it's important to you to know that she is safe. It's an important part of any sport that safety is in place for all age groups.

It will be so much easier to approach this in a calm manner and not be overly emotional about it, as this can lead to an argument straight away. If it's something you really don't want your daughter to do, then this is a tougher conversation to have, especially if your husband would love her to be involved.

It may be that she will get involved for a few weeks and then get bored, and it will be too difficult for your husband to try and keep her interested. It could also be a great way for her to learn a new skill, make new friends, and learn resilience as she deals with the falls and bumps along the way.

Ask your husband to think about the safety concerns you have, try and be ok with his decision to get her involved, especially if he understands where you are coming from in terms of safety. And if it still isn't ok with you, then you will need to have a bigger conversation.

Q. My 9-year-old son wants to play *Fortnite*, the game, and my wife says no. I go along with her, but I've played it, and it's not that bad. Obviously, I support her decision, but what is the issue?

A. If there are parents watching or listening to this and don't know what *Fortnite* is, you will soon enough. Essentially, it's a computer game that most children play: typical shoot 'em up and collecting winnings. Usually I get questions on how to stop children from playing these games, and it's unusual that I get a parent who is ok with their children playing a game. It brings up a point where the vast majority of parents will let their children play online games, and although the general speak is that we shouldn't allow this to happen, it does by thousands of children. There will always be a game, tv show or device that parents won't want their kids to be on, so it's not really about one particular game, and in this case *Fortnite*. It's more about how your child deals with playing this game, how their behaviour is, and the rules that are put in place by you as parents around the playing of this game.

If you have a 9- or 10-year-old, and they are playing this game with unlimited time restraints, and you are seeing a change in their behaviour, you need to step in as parent and control the amount of time they are playing it. If you child's behaviour is becoming aggressive, withdrawn, or just different from normal, then, as a parent, you need to do something. You will need to show your child that there has been a change in their behaviour and it is a result of playing the game. You will need to make them aware that if they start to feel frustrated or angry when playing the game, they need to stop and take a break.

There are age limits on a lot of these games, and, unfortunately, parents can be quite lax when it comes to adhering to these age limits, although they wouldn't let their child go to a movie that wasn't age appropriate. It's no different with the games; if the game is age 15 and over or 18 and over, that is because there is content in it of an adult nature and is not suitable for young children. Can your child process this content, can they understand that this is a game and not reality? All of these new experiences that your child is dealing with may be too much for them and can cause confusion and anxiety as their brains are not mature enough to deal with the more adult content.

Your children are also now in contact with people they don't know through the internet. You have no control over who they are interacting with, especially if there are no restrictions on their devices. You wouldn't allow your child to wander around with people you don't know, this is no different. Majority of people on these online games are young children, who just want to play the game, but there are also those who are there for other reasons like making contact with young children who pretend they are a similar age and befriend your child in order to get closer to them and get more personal information from them. The likelihood of this every happening is very slim, but you need to make sure that you are protecting your child so this doesn't happen, and they can be safe.

If you decide to let your child play *Fortnite*, do some background work. Make sure they are safe online and are only playing with people you know, i.e. friends. Make sure there is a time limit on their play, and they take long breaks between screen time. Regularly chat to them about the game, who's playing, and even get involved yourself.

Q. My 14 -year-old daughter wants to quit the sports she takes part in. Me and my wife feel it's important for her to stay but she is insistent. What can we do?

A. This is common especially with girls at this age and giving up sports. It happens across the board, and I, on a personal level, having girls, find it very sad to see because I think there is a society issue here where we don't give enough time and attention to the positive female role models such athletes and sports women out there. A disproportionate amount of time is given to their male counterparts, and girls find it more difficult to relate to them, and they may not see the possibilities girls may have to achieve goals in sports.

As parents, we get to a point when we don't want to have this argument with our daughter every day. We may give our daughter a note to excuse them from playing PE or let them sit out training for a week, but we may drive our son to training and matches 3 or 4 times a week and not give them the same leniency.

If your daughter is adamant that she does not want to play the sport anymore, you can agree, but only on the provision that she takes up another sport so that there is no break in activity, and it must be a sport that you agree on. It must be physically challenging and will continue to help their physical and mental health. Girls of this age who quit sports and notice their physique changing—perhaps put weight on—can sometimes turn to drastic measures to achieve the weight they would like, such as diets or choosing not to eat proper, balanced meals. I have said it before, and some people do not agree, but there is no excuse for having overweight children unless on the very rare occasion there is a health issue.

There will always be peaks and troughs in the sports they do, but it's really important that your daughter is kept physically active. Even if she quits her sport, she will need to start a new sport for at least 6 months. She may find that she misses her old sport and will return to it, but she must keep at something. There is no excuse for your child not to do PE, and I'm sure some women will not agree, but having menstrual pain is not a good enough reason not to exercise. Plenty of studies over the years have proven that engaging in exercise, perhaps just light exercise, can help with menstrual cramps.

ANXIETY

Q.

How do I talk to my child about the school shooting in America yesterday?

A.

It's a very sad and horrible thing to happen. The New York Times reported that there have only been 4 months since January 2014 where there hasn't been a shooting in a school in America. This is shocking. The people in power in America need to stop this needless killing, but that's me just sounding off.

You may not be living in America, but your children are going to be talking about this at home or in school. When Donald Trump was elected as president, I was asked at a number of parenting talks, 'how do I explain a person like Donald Trump becoming the president of America?' With all the media coverage on Donald Trump it has become apparent to even the youngest people in our lives that he is not a nice person and shouldn't be someone to rule a country. This media coverage has gone worldwide and is not just concentrated in America. With that, so much news comes out of America and especially tragedies such as school shootings. News like this can become very worrying for our children who perhaps cannot, at this stage, imagine their school being different to any other school in the world and may feel that this is something that could possibly happen to them too.

You need to be able to explain to your child that this will not happen in their school, that they are safe and that you live in a safe country. Unfortunately, it is very difficult for children to understand the awful stories on the news as it seems it is everywhere. It can lead to anxiety in your children and make them weary of everyday life.

The most important thing you can do is try and filter out as much news as possible, they don't need to know about everything that's going on. If they do ask questions about certain news topics, answer them as sympathetically as possible without adding to their fears. Keep your children safe and happy, just concern yourself with their little world. If you feel your child is becoming overly anxious, you may need to seek outside help. You can always talk to their school or a professional or you can drop me an e-mail to discuss your worries.

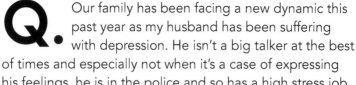

Q. Our family has been facing a new dynamic this past year as my husband has been suffering with depression. He isn't a big talker at the best of times and especially not when it's a case of expressing his feelings, he is in the police and so has a high stress job where he sees people at their worst on a daily occurrence but can't talk to people outside of work about it. We've been working through it and he has finally opened up a bit more to me and his parents and he is now seeing a counsellor weekly.

So, my question is if you have any advice for parents dealing with depression or for their partners. What's been difficult is not always having the support I had in the past with parenting because sometimes he is just in such a dark place he isn't able to be as present as he was with our kids, and that's hard for him, too, he has always been a very hands-on dad and completely invested in our children's lives. For me it's tough because I'm trying to keep the peace and balance in the home, so it isn't causing more stress and trying to be emotionally available for our kids and my husband while being emotionally exhausted myself worrying about him. Our daughters are young, 4 and 2, and while they are too young to completely understand the situation I'm well aware that they can pick up on how we feel and on any tension or anxiety in the home and the last thing in the world I would want is for us to take our tiredness and hurt on them or the opposite and burn ourselves out completely by trying to over compensate.

I'll admit I don't know a lot about depression, this past year has been a steep learning curve for me, but since mental health has recently been gradually more accepted and talked about publicly, I just wondered if you had a course specifically for dealing with parenting with mental health or if you had some advice, I think it could probably benefit a lot of families out there as I'm sure we aren't alone.

Anxiety

A. As a parent, you want to look after your children and keep them safe and happy, but at the same time, your relationship with your husband came first and is the reason why you have two lovely daughters. It's positive now that he is getting help to deal with his depression. It's not an easy thing to do and sometimes we don't fully understand depression and we can sometimes look at people and question why they can't get out of bed and start their day or why they don't want to involve themselves in day to day life.

It's great he is getting help, but the other issue is what about you, how are you coping? You may feel guilt for having these feelings and thoughts as it is your husband who is going through the depression. It's very difficult for you to try and keep the train on the tracks for all your family members and yourself and stay positive. The children will be ok, they are far more resilient than we give them credit for. As children, they will most likely remember all the good times with you and your husband and won't remember the bumps in the road. Also, children are very forgiving and if they understand and know that you and your husband love each other and equally love them, they will understand the rougher times.

In terms of support for you, you need to find the support you need. You can't be expected to keep all the balls in the air all the time, this is unrealistic and may lead you feeling under more pressure. Your day-to-day life will not turn into chaos if you let a couple of the balls drop every now and again. Life in busy households has its fluctuations, weeks that are great and weeks that don't quite go to plan. You need to look after your mental health and wellbeing, too. If it means you need to get a babysitter or a family member to look after the children while you go for a walk or an exercise class, so be it, or if you need to get professional help also do that. You need to put measures in place to look after yourself, too. If you don't, you will carry on and push through it all until it comes to a point when you just can't cope any longer and then there is feelings of guilt, illness, and a cycle of worry that the day-to-day routine will not keep going. You need to take the little breaks, times to yourself every day or week that will help you keep your head clear and focused.

Encourage your husband to have 10 to 15 minutes with your kids every day or at different points during the day to have some fun and catch up on what's going on with them. You are not asking him to look after them for 3 hours which could be overwhelming for him. Giving him small, fun bursts with the kids will make him feel better about the time he spends with them, it will be a positive result all round. Talk to your husband about introducing this time with the children and give it a go, if it doesn't work that's ok.

Look at the activities your kids are doing. If they are in the house a lot and there is an atmosphere, get them out. Take a walk, play a game outside. Your kids will remember this more than being in the house feeling upset or worried.

We all make mistakes and don't get it right every time, and it's ok for our children to see this and for them to know that it can be fixed or worked out, together as a family. Everyone makes mistakes, in all walks of life but nothing is unfixable.

Q.

I've a 12-year-old in 6th class. We noticed he was a little less interested in school this year— off sick a few times. Figured out he was anxious about it being his last year in primary school and transition into secondary. Mix that with hormones it's makes things a little testing. Any advice on this transition?

A.

It's something that is very common among children this age who are going from primary to secondary school. They are going from being the eldest and most respected pupils in the school to all of a sudden being on the bottom of the heap again and the students in sixth year are practically grown adults. This can seem quite intimidating. There will be a lot more that your child will need to take responsibility for plus the extra burden of lockers, moving classes, where to go. The first thing you can do is have some small general conversations about the move to secondary, nothing planned, just casual while you are in the car or out for a walk and see how he is feeling about the transition. He may say it's fine and no more, but he might open up and let you know how he is feeling. If you keep the conversations light and don't press him if he doesn't want to talk about it, he is more likely to come back to you at a future point and maybe tell you exactly how he is feeling.You could also talk to the school he is in and see if they are planning on doing any trips to the local secondary schools so the new students can have a look around and familiarise themselves with the layout. If this isn't the case, get in touch with the new school and see if you can visit it sometime.

Start to talk about all the positives of going to secondary school. Subjects that he will be interested in, and that there is a lot more freedom in secondary school. If he is anxious and it is continuing to affect his day-to-day life, it may be time to consult with a professional to get him some help. You can tell him everything will be ok, and he can tell himself the same, but that doesn't get rid of the worry of the unknown, which can escalate and become something more serious. He has attached an emotion to how he feels about going to secondary school and it's sticking, and he is unable to logically sort this out himself. Give him the space to try and figure this out, keep talking to him about the positives of going to secondary school, and if it doesn't appear to be getting better then seek professional help. It probably won't take many sessions to help him deal with the anxiety and he will have gained tools on how to deal with situations that may make him anxious in the future.

Q. My 5-year-old child started school last September. After every school holiday (i.e. Christmas, Easter) they are very anxious about returning to school and it lasts for most of the first week back. Have you any suggestions as to what we can do to help?

A. This can be very distressing for parents to see their child becoming anxious about going to school. We want our children to feel safe and happy when they leave our home to go to school and to have the best experience there as possible. That may not always be the case, of course, it can take some children a while to settle back into a new routine—especially a school routine when the days start earlier; it's more structured and bedtime is earlier too! Children coming off holidays have enjoyed more sleep, more playtime and being allowed to stay up past the normal bedtime. All of this can have a knock-on effect on how they integrate back into the school term routine.

You can perhaps start the school routine: i.e. earlier bedtimes, up a bit earlier in the mornings, a couple of days before they go back. Ask them the day before what they would like for lunch the next day and structure the time if possible. They may become a bit unsettled about this, but have conversations about the good things about school, what they are looking forward to most about being back. Chat about friends, telling their teacher about the holidays, and what you got up to. This routine is very new for your child, even if they were in preschool before this. School is different, the structure and expectations are different, so it may take some children a couple of years before they really get the hang of it and go off happily.

Have the conversation with your child about their feelings; it's a really good idea to put a name on it for your child. There is no point in worrying yourself sick about it and trying to fix the situation if you are not talking to your child about how they are feeling. You can use very simple language to help them to describe what they are feeling. Their tummy might be sore or feel tight, it might feel like they have giant butterflies instead of the small fluttery one when you feel excited. They might have a pain in their head or feel tired as they are over processing all their thoughts. Ask are they feeling upset about going back and let them know that's it's perfectly normal to feel that way, even we as adults feel like that when we go back to work or back to the normal routine after holidays. Talk about this, share the experience as it normalises this for your child which allows them to open up and chat about how they are feeling, which then helps to sort out the emotions and ultimately learn how to deal with them to the point where they nearly don't exist at all.

Nearly all children go through this and learn to grow out of it. Of course, if it's something that only seems to be getting worse even though you have tried the above, then you may need to delve deeper and see if there are any issues in school. Perhaps a chat with their teacher might highlight something that is going on. If there isn't anything going on in school, and they are still highly anxious, it may be worth seeking some professional help. It's difficult at this stage to know if this is something that will be long term. You need to try out a few processes at home, see does this help, and allow a couple of months to pass before seeking more help. Sometimes it just takes a bit of time and there are no quick-fix solutions.

Q. Hi I'm a young mum and have a beautiful 19-month-old son. I felt quite anxious and worried about looking after him and me being isolated when he was born. I joined mum and toddler groups in the local community hall and following some parenting bloggers online, but I've found recently, looking back, they caused me more anxiety and stress and I would go to a meeting or read something and it would just make me feel worse about my situation. Is there something wrong with me, as everyone always seems to suggest these groups as a really good thing for new mothers.

A. This can be quite controversial situation. We are regularly told that we should engage with people and be sociable especially after the birth of a first child so as to have a connection with similar people and have that support. Sometimes it's ok not to feel that way or to perhaps feel better off for not getting involved in these groups. It may not have been the right group for you; we are all different and enjoy different company. You went and tried it out, but if you are having some difficulty with your own child it can be hard and worrying to listen to parents who chat about how well their baby is eating, sleeping, moving about, and you can doubt your own ability as a parent. We all develop at different stages and as long as there is nothing out of the normal wrong with your baby, they will hit all the milestones in their own time, and the most important thing for you to do is enjoy them when they do happen in your own time and without worrying what others are doing.

With the increase in so called 'experts' online blogging about their experiences or putting pictures up of every day their baby has lived so far, it is very easy to get sucked in, and, unfortunately, what has happened is that new parents look to these pages for advice instead of perhaps first listening to their own natural inbuilt instincts. If you are going to all your check-ups and doctors or nurses are happy with your baby's development, well that's fantastic. Enjoy your baby and the time with them, it goes so quickly. Have a couple of close friends or family members close by when you need a moan or need a couple of hours free, everyone needs it.

Being a parent can be daunting, nobody gets it right every day, we all mess up at some point, but as long as your child is loved, cared for, and happy you are doing a great job. Take one day at a time, enjoy the little daily triumphs and don't be too hard on yourself.

Q. My children are constantly begging us to get a dog. We have no pets as I'm not a huge animal lover. As a child I was bitten by a dog and I can feel uncomfortable around big dogs. I don't want to disappoint the kids but I'm quite apprehensive.

A. Kids love pets and pets love kids, but it has to work for everyone in the family. It's very common for parents who have had a bad experience with a dog to feel protective of their own children as they feel the same may happen again. The first thing about having a pet is that it gives a level of responsibility to your children that they can learn valuable life lessons from as they have to take care of a living being. I know there are probably a number of parents who are now saying they have to take care of the pet all the time and it's not the children, but they would have been involved a bit and they can see what it is involved in looking after an animal.

There is so much fun and joy from having a pet and as it is yours, you can train it and make sure it behaves well around children, other people. It is also a way to help your children experience death for possibly the first time and how to deal with those emotions.

You can always start small with something like a goldfish, get the kids involved and then maybe look into different dog breeds that might suit you best. Talk to friends and family about their pets and get some idea of what is involved. If these feelings of fear are affecting you more than you realised, it may be worth going and talking to someone about it. The likelihood of the same thing happening to your children is very slim and I'm sure you don't want to pass those fears onto your children and then possibly onto grandchildren in the future. Best of luck!

Q. Both my husband and I work full time. We have 2 young children in a child minders 5 days a week. It's breaking my heart missing out on so much of their lives. We have a lot of outgoings, but we don't have an extravagant lifestyle. How can I be ok with leaving my kids every day?

A. There a lot of parents who are in this situation, it's really tough. You have as people before you got married or had children decided to have a career which is a really important part of your life. You have reached certain salary levels and you have lived a lifestyle that has been supported by your wages. Now having children there is an additional element that needs to be included in your outgoings plus you have probably moved house with a larger mortgage, cars.

There is now the pressure for both of you to continue the lifestyle you have and keep working full time to support this. This now means that you will have to find childcare for your children out of the house as, like many parents, you may not have the luxury of having family close by to help out with the minding. It is heart-breaking for you to leave your children for so long every day and also the amount of money that you have to pay to the childminders to look after your children.

If this issue is really making life difficult for you, you need to look at your job and your wages and see are they really worth it. If you are paying nearly all of your wages to a childminder, travel to and from work, perhaps it might be worth looking for part time work or take a break from yours or your partner's job for a few years until your children are in school. Is there a possibility that you could work 3 or 4 days a week?

Before you make any decisions, the most important thing to do now is sit down with your partner and talk through your best scenario in terms of work and looking after your children. Figure out what your monthly income might be and then go through all your monthly outgoings—everything—and see where you could cut out or cut back and reduce your outgoings. You would be amazed at the amount of money you spend on nothing!! It might mean takeaway once a month, not so many meals out or shopping in a different supermarket. Also, when it comes to changing your insurances or energy suppliers, you might be better off shopping around and reducing those monthly bills too.

There are always ways to save money and to make these situations work out especially if it's what you really want in the long term. You'll be amazed at how well it works out and you'll look back and wonder why you didn't do it sooner. Sometimes being with our children is far more important than the materialistic things in our lives, it will create a sense of contentment and happiness and in a few years you may be at the point where you choose to go back to work or work in a different field that suits your new lifestyle.

Q. My son is heading into secondary school in September and I'm really feeling anxious about this. He seems fine about it, but I'm just so worried about him going into an environment and the pressures that come with it. Are there any techniques you can suggest to help me deal with my anxiety?

A. So let's look at the anxiety side of how you are feeling about your son. Anxiety is usually grown out of worrying about the future, it's not about what you are thinking right now or the present day. What happens is that we start to catastrophise everything and turn it into a disaster. We fall into a pit of worrying about them studying, doing drugs, drinking too much, or falling in with the wrong friends. Most of this will not happen, and a lot of it is part of going to secondary school, making mistakes and learning about life. No one ever thinks about the best-case scenario, that they will love this experience, they will achieve so much, and be so happy in secondary school. The reality is it will probably land somewhere in the middle, with ups and downs. Be happy that you have gotten him this far and that he is doing his best, as are you.

You need to give him trust and let him figure out this new part of his life. He needs to know that you will be there for him to help him figure out the tougher stuff, especially if things don't always work out the way he thought they would. You will be able to sit down and figure things out together and help him to come up the best solution for him, just let him know that you will be there. He needs to know that it's ok to make mistakes, it happens to everyone all of the time and they are a great way of learning for the future.

To help you deal with the worry and anxiety perhaps have a journal and write down what it is that is making you feel this way. Then put it down and come back to it later and see if you still feel that way or try and rationalise how you were feeling earlier with realistic outcomes. This will help you to take control of your feelings and the emotions involved with the next chapter of your son's life. It's ok to let him know how you are feeling, that you are excited and nervous for him at the same time. He may be a bit embarrassed by this but that's ok. Chat to your partner or friends and family and let them know how you are feeling, not for answers but just generally how you are feeling.

If this isn't working and the anxiety is taking over your life and how you cope with everyday life, you may need to see your GP or a professional counsellor, there could also be other things that are going on too. Don't be afraid to seek professional help or perhaps look at some mindfulness techniques you could use. One in particular is Headspace, which I have used myself and it helped a lot.

The important thing is to remember that what you are feeling is not your son's fault, it is how you are feeling about his next step in life and how you are going to deal with it. Sometimes you can project your feelings onto your child and say that they are feeling anxious, but in fact they're not, it's you.

Dealing with how you are feeling will make this next stage more enjoyable and help you to deal with the challenges if and when they come up. Be proud that you have gotten your son to this next exciting stage of his life.

Q. My son is starting school next week and I'm a nervous wreck. We've been so close and had so much fun over the past 5 years, and what makes it worse is that he has to get the bus. It's not a long journey, but I just want to make sure he's okay. How can I get rid of this feeling of anxiety?

A. It's such a major milestone in so many family's lives when their child starts primary school, this alone can be an anxious time, but then putting them on the bus when they still seem so small can add to that anxiety. A lot of people will remember their first day in school, the excitement, the butterflies, maybe even some tears, and it's the same feelings for the parents, too, except you are trying to hold back the tears until they've gone. It's ok to feel nervous or anxious around this time, it's a huge step in hour child's development and the months fly by as soon as they get into a more structured year.

Give yourself a break, it's ok to feel the way you are feeling, but if you don't deal with your own anxieties, you may pass them on to your child and this can sometimes change the way your child will feel about school or the school bus. Your son will be fine in school and on the bus. There may be a couple of days at the start when he's upset or not telling you what happened as he's trying to process all the new things in his life. This will change and he'll be a happy child going to school every day. Teachers have changed since when we went to school, they are so well trained and able to deal with the majority of children who come through their door. If they are in any way concerned about your son in school, they will let you know as for them it's better to deal with any issues sooner rather than later.

Your son will be learning so much, making so many friends and having fun in a safe, secure environment.

The bus will be fine, too, as the bus drivers are very experienced and well-equipped to deal with any issues that may arise. Child safety on buses is of paramount importance to bus drivers, this is their livelihood, too, and they take their responsibilities very seriously. The teachers, too, are highly qualified and skilled and want to create a good learning environment for your child while also having fun and being safe.

Once you have the first few days over you will start to feel less anxious, and this is a time when you can look at yourself and have time for yourself. If you are not working out of the home this is a time to look at doing something new for yourself or focusing on house issues that you needed more time to deal with.

Distraction is a great way of keeping yourself positive and busy while your child is at school and this could be a great time for further development for you.

It's a really positive time for you and your child, enjoy it and all the wonderful new and exciting experiences it will bring to your family.

Q. My 19-year-old son is finished school, doesn't know what he wants to do. He sleeps late and lazes around the house a lot. When I talk to him about getting a job, he says he's on it and not to be putting him under stress. This situation is really getting me down as I thought when he finished school, the stress would be less. Any advice?

A. Adult children are in the home a lot longer than when we were growing up. There is less opportunity for them to work and start to live their own independent lives. The cost of living and rent, has risen so much and it is harder for them to be independent at an earlier age.

Having an adult child in the house changes the family dynamic as you need to recognise that your child is an adult and therefore the boundaries put in place have now changed. Your child also needs to respect that they are still living in your home and need to contribute like all the other adults i.e. rent, if possible, bills, housework. Your child is being fed and sheltered and should not be allowed to take advantage of this.

You will need to sit down with your child and have an adult conversation with him about what his plans are now that he is finished school but still living at home. Discuss job opportunities, and if he feels there is nothing there for him, offer some help but give him a time frame to find work, be it 2 weeks, 3 weeks, but if after this time he hasn't managed to get a job, he needs to help more with the day-to-day household work. He needs to be up, cleaning, shopping, minding other siblings.

Get him involved more in the daily financial side of the household so he is aware of the bills that need to be paid, the cost of feeding the house for a week. This isn't in any way set out to scare him, but if he isn't going out to work, he can learn so much from being in the home that will help him when he does get a job or goes to college and needs to fend for himself. It is our job as parents of adult children to make sure that they are equipped to go out and live their own lives and not pamper and do everything for them because they are still living in the home. Like when our children are young, we teach them so much around what is right and wrong and helping them to do things for themselves, and it's no different when they get older. There will always be work, it may not be the type of work your son wants to do, but the satisfaction of getting your first wage that you have earnt all by yourself is a great motivator to keep working and the best bit is getting to spend it! Any work your son does will show future employers he is willing and able to work, and this is much more appealing to employers than people who have no experience.

This is not the time for you to be mapping out his life plan, we all change and have many different jobs and careers before we find what we really want to do. Your job at the moment is to get him on the ladder, earning a wage and getting him to contribute to the family household if he continues to live with you.

He may need your help and that's fine, it's what you are there for, and hopefully this will help in the long term. If he doesn't get a job, look at some voluntary work. You may have to get him up every morning to go to work, but it will be worth it in the end. So have the conversation, tell him you are there to help, and keep at it.

BEING A PARENT

Q.

How do I build resilience in my child?

A.

Building resilience in children can be difficult. We talk about wanting our children to be confident, have good self-esteem and be resilient, but how do we encourage these traits to develop in our children?

All humans, adults, and children need to feel that they have something worthwhile to contribute to the world, that they are needed and are important. Starting to build resilience in your child can begin with as simple a task as giving them responsibility for something or someone like a pet or giving them jobs/chores to do around the house. Learning to take responsibility, carrying out the task, and be praised for the good work achieved can start to build confidence in your child, which can then in turn build resilience.

I remember receiving my first wage when I was about 10 or 11 years old and going home and telling my parents that I didn't need their financial support anymore, I was so happy and confident with myself and believed that I had made it!

Give your child responsibility.

A lot of young adults or 'Millennials' are told they have been wrapped in a bubble and are unable to cope with today's pressures. This is not their fault. If they were given the proper tools to deal with life in the first place, they could deal with these pressures with more confidence.

When children are learning to walk, we allow them to get up, fall, get up again, fall again, until they get their balance and take those first precious steps. All through their lives we need to treat each new experience they have in the same way. We need to step back and allow them to make the mistakes, learn from them, and try again, but always be present in the background when they come to us for help or advice. If we as parents continue to do everything for our children and protect them from the 'falls' in life, they will never gain the tools to deal with life's pressures as they get older.

Some lessons are difficult. If you had a 6 or 7-year-old child who was being bullied in school, your first instinct as a parent would be to protect your child by any means possible. But if this meant becoming a bully, too, towards the parents of the child that was bullying, or even worse the bully themselves, you would not be teaching your child a sensible solution to the problem.

One way to deal with this might be to ask your child if they had any solutions on how to deal with it. Let them feel they are in control of the situation and how to get out of it. If they can't come up with anything, then it's your time to help them. You could come up with a solution and act it out with your child, so it becomes a familiar situation for them. It may not solve the problem, but it may give them the confidence to stand up for themselves and show the bully that they are a lot more confident than they first thought.

Don't always jump in to help your child (unless of course it is a dangerous situation for them). Learning is a part of life and sometimes it is painful.

Q. My 4-year-old just asked how we made her. What do you recommend you say to a child this age? I told her I would tell her another time. I'm such a wimp!

A. There are some questions that parents dread coming from their children and one of them is "Where did I come from." Everything is about giving them information that is age appropriate. She doesn't need to know exactly how she was conceived, but you can talk about how you and her dad love each other and when parents love each other they can make a baby. Hopefully this will do and she won't ask how. You can always tell her that you will go into more details when she is older and that for now all she needs to know is that she was made from love. Most children of your daughter's age will be happy with this answer.

Don't make it difficult on yourself by feeling that you need to provide a lengthy answer. Being a parent can be as tough as you want to make it! Sometimes overthinking things and wondering if you do or don't do something or say something will have a long-term effect on your child. All children who develop into adults will have issues regardless of how you bring them up. All you can do at any one time in your child's life is your best, no one gets it right every time. If something does come up later in life for your child or young adult that may be a result of something you did or didn't do, all you can do is apologise and help them through it. Try your best every day and take some pressure off yourself.

Q. Since having our 8-month-old baby my relationship with my husband has taken a back seat. I know he's frustrated, but I'm so tired and when the baby sleeps, I just want to sleep too. I want to kick start our relationship but don't know where to start. Any advice?

A. When a couple become pregnant there is the excitement of telling everyone and looking forward to your new family member. You are not thinking about the lack of sleep that's coming your way. If you think about a day when you were really tired before having kids and multiply that by 100 you still wouldn't get close to the tiredness felt when you have children, especially young babies. It's part of early family life and everyone goes through it.

Sometimes when you are that tired you just need to concentrate on one step at a time, one hour at a time, to get through that first 18+ months of little sleep. Don't be too hard on yourself.

When it comes to your relationship, I would say to a couple that you got together in the first place for a reason, not just to have children. You had things in common, you enjoyed spending time together. It's ok to want to get that relationship back, not just sex but also the friendship. After a long day of looking after children, pets, you probably don't want to have to talk to your partner, you just want to switch off, but maybe even just have the conversation about your relationship. Let him know that you are aware that your relationship has taken a back seat and it's not what you want. Express how tired you are and I'm sure he would understand. Look at trying to get a night out together or even a cuppa coffee during the day. Try and get back to spending a bit of time together just the two of you. Sex in a relationship after having a baby can become less frequent or stop completely, it's not unusual. Perhaps pick a night during the week to have sex, it may seem really strange to schedule a day, but it might kick start a more regular pattern as you experience that closeness again.

Have the conversation, ask is he frustrated. Don't be offended or annoyed if he says he is, you both need to air what's going on. Try and get some adult time, not every week, but something to look forward to. If you can't get out, instead of watching tv, maybe put some music on, have a chat, and connect with each other again. Hopefully these small steps will help to get you through this challenging time and keep your relationship with your partner strong.

Q. Why do kids lie?

A. Why does anyone lie? Because they don't want to get into trouble. This question made me think about what adults expect of kids. You wonder why they can't just do what they are asked and continue to do the same thing repeatedly although you've asked them not to. But adults all over the world do the same thing and we don't give them as much hassle as we do our kids. We have an expectation that kids should understand things the same way adults do, but this isn't possible as their brains haven't developed enough to understand certain concepts.

What is your child lying about? Is it just a small white lie that could be overlooked, a battle that you don't really need to get into with your child? If it's lying about a bigger matter, something that may cause harm or danger to your child, or it's a behaviour that is happening too often, then a conversation will need to be had with your child. You need to ask why they are lying, and if it continues, then consequences may need to be put in place to discourage the behaviour. But don't forget they are kids, with loads of learning to do, and just don't want to get into trouble!

Q. We are a young couple thinking of starting a family and would like some advice on how best to jointly parent our children. We had different upbringings with good and bad elements and would like to get a good balance for both of us.

A. It's great to hear that you are thinking about how you will parent your children although you don't have any yet. It's good to discuss your own upbringing and what you and your partner would like to take out of it for your own children. No one sits down and plans how they are going to bring up a child. At the beginning, all you are concerned with is keeping the baby fed and happy, one day at a time, one step at a time. As adults we make plans about how we are going to buy a house, a car, or afford our wedding, but never plan how we are going to bring up our kids until one day we have a toddler who is acting up a bit and one parent gives them a slap on the behind and the other is shocked. It may have been something that happened in their house growing up as a form of discipline, but not in the other's, and the couple may not have discussed whether or not they would slap their children.

First look at how you both were brought up and make a list of the elements that your parents used to bring you up, the good and bad. Have a chat, discussion about how you would like to bring up your child. There are no definites in parenting, you don't know how your child will develop. You may have an idea, but if this doesn't come to fruition, it is good to sit down and make a parenting plan so at least both of you are on the same page when you start putting the plan in place.

Sometimes we put measures in place that work really well for a while, but as your child grows up and changes and pushes the boundaries, you, too, will need to change your parenting approach even though you may feel unsettled as it seems like it's back to square one again.

We can get overwhelmed and feel that things aren't working, but you need to sit down and look at the behaviour, what it is that you are struggling with. Sometimes one parent has a different issue than you, something that doesn't bother one parent but maybe the other, and you need to accept each other's feelings on a situation. Discuss how you can solve a situation, be on the same team, and help each other. If it doesn't work, try something else. Take the time to try out a new way to resolve a problem with your child and stick to it for a few days but be on the same page. Parents need both parents to be united to get the best outcome for everyone in the family.

Q. How do you keep your composure, and a straight face, when you are trying to discipline or discuss something with your child, and they respond to you in some way that just makes you want to laugh?

A. This is something that happens to so many parents across the world. You know you have to reprimand them or correct them in some way, but you are laughing on the inside and trying so hard for it not to escape as you tackle the tricky issue of discipline! There are some times you have to hold it in, take a deep breath, and get on with it. You may need to leave the room and return when you have the giggles under control. Remember if you do laugh in front of them that they won't take anything you say seriously!

Q. My kids take up most of my time. I have no energy and all I want to do in the evening is sit down and relax. I've been putting on weight and this is worrying me. How do I get the balance between allowing myself to switch off and keep fit?

Being A Parent

A. We are so tired and the thought of getting up and having to exercise can seem like such a pain when all you want to do is sit on the sofa with a cup of tea and maybe even a little biscuit or a little bar of chocolate! This is when the weight can sneak up on you and you all of a sudden wonder why your clothes don't fit, or you have little energy. Not exercising and having a little treat every day can lead to weight creeping on, and this not only effects your physical appearance but also your mental health.

You want to be fit and healthy for yourself and also to give a good example to your children. Children learn just as much from what they see as what they hear! We continually tell them what they can and can't eat and that they need to exercise, and we don't do the same ourselves, it gives a very confusing message to our children.

Even if your kids are going to bed and you are going out to exercise, let them know you are exercising. Have a chat at the table the next day that you were out with your friends at a class or a jog. Let them know you are exercising, and go and do it, plus it's really good for your mental health. Being in a house all day looking after your family can be hard work on your mental health. Get out of the house, get some fresh air, go to a class with friends, and have a good moan about the things that drove you nuts earlier! You will feel so much better and this will have a knock on effect with your energy levels, your patience to deal with family issues, your appearance, and all this good will make you less likely to reach for the treats at the end of the day or sit on the sofa watching TV for a couple of hours.

Try and make some healthy changes in your eating, nothing drastic. Just don't fall into the trap of feeling you deserve the bar of chocolate or biscuits because you exercised that day. Have a day once a week that is your treat day and look forward to the bar of chocolate. You wouldn't give your kids treats every day, so don't do it yourself. If you struggle with sweet treats in the house get rid of them. I can't have treats in my house because I will eat them all, I have a really sweet tooth and if I'm not going to give them to the children, I will eat them myself! We have a treat day once a week. I found before, I was putting on weight and not feeling good about myself, so the treats went, and that sorted one aspect of my health.

Commit to meet friends for an exercise class or going walking, jogging. If you make a commitment to someone else to exercise, you are more likely to stick with it. Look at what you are doing now and how you think you could change this. Little steps that are manageable and life changing not just for a few weeks.

Q. Where can I sell my children…I've had enough of them!!

A. I'd say you are the only parent in the world to ever experience this!!! I've heard eBay, Facebook Market Place, and Amazon shop if need be. All are popular options.

Don't give your children away even if they are annoying you, you annoy them too!

Q. I'm a stay-at-home mum with 2 children of school-going age. They have homework and after school activities nearly every day, and with these also comes a lot of contact from the school and people running activities. I'm sometimes overwhelmed with all the information and events, dates, to remember. My partner is out working with an early start and sometimes not home until late evening. He is the sole financial contributor to the household and my decision to stay at home was made jointly. He is very hands on at the weekends and I tend not to discuss the craziness of the week with him in the evenings as it's usually a time for us both to switch off. I feel that if the Monday-to-Friday routine continues the way it is, I will become run down and then possibly angry and resentful towards my children and husband. I need help to take the pressure off during the week but not sure how this is possible. Any advice?

A. This will resonate with a lot of parents; it happens in many households. When I was growing up this was normal, many households had mum at home and dad out working. When we were doing activities, we were probably a bit older and walked to most of them with our friends. There wasn't a huge amount of time commitment from parents back then, they didn't hang around and watch us train or even come to matches. For a lot of parents now there is an expectation that they will stay around and commit to driving children to several different activities. It's one of the advantages for our children that they are experiencing so many well-run activities and different sports, that were not available before.

Parents who stay at home sometimes feel that they need to justify the fact that they stay at home as there can be the perception that their lives are not as difficult as those parents who go out to work and then need deal with home life, too. This, of course, isn't the case as the parent at home takes on nearly all the household and family chores/activities. School and after school life for our children takes a huge amount of organisation, and there is also the feeling of having to present a relaxed, calm environment for the other parent who has been out working all day, which is very difficult. Taking on most the house and parenting roles is extremely exhausting and having no or little time off from this can lead to feelings of resentment, frustration, tiredness and a loss of your own self.

You need to try and sit down with your partner when it's quiet and you can talk. Perhaps get out for a meal together, time alone to discuss how you are feeling. Prepare what you would like to say and the possible outcome. That may seem a bit prescriptive, but if this is an issue that is bothering you and making you feel down, then it needs to be discussed properly in the time you have. Together come up with a list of possible solutions that you can both work on but don't put pressure on each other to get it 100% straight away. It may take time or tweaking to some of the plan, but at least if you are facing it together and the parent at home knows there is support, this is a great start to putting a more permanent solution in place. The solution needs to be easily knitted into your family routine as it is at the moment, it could be as simple as trying to get home 15 minutes earlier to put the kids to bed a couple of nights a week. It will take a bit of work, but if it can be achieved, it could make big differences to your busy day and stronger relationship between you and your partner.

Q. Not really a parenting question, but my mum is in her 50's and does nothing for herself. She was a stay-at-home mum and always looked after the family. We are all grown up now, and it seems like she's lost her purpose in life. We've tried getting her out and about, but all she wants to do is stay at home and clean the house every day. What can we do to make her realise she is still young and can do so much?

A. This has become more common. Parents who have been out working are used to being out and about and getting involved in everyday life. Sometimes for people who have spent a lot of their time at home raising their children it is the only world they really know and are comfortable in. For some they feel that their next step is to wait until grandchildren come along and be there to help mind them for their children.

You need to start having conversations with your mum about her interests, things she likes to do. Maybe then gently start letting her know about courses/classes you've seen that she might be interested in. Perhaps if she takes something up, keep interested in it and ask her questions, and then if there is a further course, encourage her to do it. Look for local groups for coffee mornings that you could perhaps go to with her until she feels comfortable going by herself. See what her neighbours are up to, does she have a relationship with any of them? Local charity shops are always looking for volunteers to help. This is a great way to meet people with no commitment, but you will be helping in the community and it gets her out of the house.

Invite her out a bit more, especially to events that she will be interested in. Sometimes it's the unknown that can make you a little anxious and nervous about change, but your mum has already done one of the toughest jobs already and that's raising a family.

Q. My brother recently gave me a funny birthday card and I didn't take any real notice of it. My 5-year-old just asked me what a "tit" is, and I've was completely stuck for an answer. Please tell me I'll be able deal with this stuff better as he gets older and asks the harder ones?

A. Birthday cards, we get them, we laugh at them, and we put them up, and then eventually our children start to notice them, too, and learn to read and need them explained! You could always tell your child that a "tit" is a type of bird, and that there are many different types and colours.

Usually when this happens for the first time, you can get caught off-guard and don't have an answer. You'll be more prepared next time to deal with the innuendo of the cards you get in the following years. Some things you can explain, other things may be a bit more adult, so either don't put the cards up, or give them an innocent enough answer until the time comes when they are old enough for the real explanation.

Q. I was recently looking for a photo of my daughter and I fell into a black hole of old photos from when all my kids were small. Why do we never print out photos out anymore?

A. It's amazing how many pictures we have stored on computers, phones. Everybody, why not go and make a photo album for your kids, one or two photos from each year, and give it to them when they leave the house? Lovely memories for them to take with them and remember their childhood—the good and bad!

Q. My 12-year-old child is going back to school in a few weeks and the cost of sending him to school has gone through the roof. On top of that, he's suddenly become obsessed with brand names and only wants branded clothes, school bag. I don't want him to feel left out, but at the same time, we don't have the money to just buy tons of brand names. Any advice?

A. Branded clothes, brands are fantastic, and anyone who thinks that big name companies don't advertise their products specifically to young children or teenagers, you need to take another look. They are aware that if you can introduce a young person to a brand early on, they are more likely to stick with this brand for life and they are guaranteed income.

It's important that we manage our families in terms of brands and the reality of whether or not you as a family can afford to buy these products for your children. Please do not put yourself under financial pressure or go without certain necessary items for you or your family in order to keep your child happy with certain branded goods. That's not the way life works; we don't get what we want all the time so we have to learn to not have the latest items of clothing, game, until we have saved for it, or it comes down in price in a sale, or ask for it for a birthday or Christmas. There are big money items I would love to have but can't as I don't have the means to purchase them.

Maybe there can be a comprise. Perhaps you can afford to buy your son one branded item for school (i.e. school bag, trainers or a hoodie). You need to let them know that this is what you can afford as a family and that if they would like something else you can give them a list of things that need to be done around the house and they can earn the money for other items. They are old enough to understand how money is earned and spent, budgets and household bills. They may not want to hear it, or think you are making too big a deal about it, but it's the reality of life. You are teaching them a valuable lesson, and they will see the importance of money and how it is spent.

Even if you could afford all the things they wanted, what would you be teaching your child about life? They wouldn't learn about the value of money and work and money. How will they know themselves how to survive when they become adults? Try to compromise, buy one item and if he complains about this, then he doesn't get anything, and he will have to save and get the item himself. No parent wants their child to be left out, and of course you want them to fit in with their peers, so compromise is good and healthy relations around money and budgeting. will be established between you and your son.

If you give into your child at this age now and buy him all the things he wants, it will never stop, and it will become more difficult for you financially because as they get older, everything becomes more expensive.

Q. Have you any suggestions on how to teach my kids about money management?

A. Depending on the age they are, you can start to have the conversation about saving money, especially if there is something they would like to buy outside of the normal birthday, Christmas gift time. Bring them down to the bank or post office to open a savings account where they put their money every week, and they will be very surprised in a few weeks' time how much money they have saved. The sense of self-worth they will have should encourage them to keep saving for the next item they would like to buy.

If your child is younger, a piggy bank is great, and they can pop their coins in there. It's also a great time to get your children doing a bit more around the house, especially things like washing cars, which will earn them a few more euro to add to their pot and introduce a good sense of work and wage to them without expecting them to do 8 hour days!

Q. I'm am expecting my second child and I'm 21. While I'm happy and excited, I'm worried that life is passing me by and I'm putting my potential career on hold and by the time the kids are old enough for me to go to work, I won't be employable. What can I do to keep my career open?

A. In the big scheme of things, and I don't mean this in a patronizing way, you are still very young at 21. You've been working for the last 5 years and you will have a possible 40 plus working years ahead of you, so there is loads of time for you achieve what you would like for your future. This, of course, will be hard work especially having two small children, but it is certainly achievable.

If you are working part time or a stay-at-home parent, is this what you would like to continue to do until your children are older? Life is long and so is our working career, and for many people, our careers change many times. Sometimes it is just a different direction in the same field, or for some it's a totally different career later in life. Our career potential is so different nowadays, most people don't spend all their working life in one job.

Being young and having time is a great opportunity for you to think about what you may like to do as a possible future career. Write down what interests you or what you would like to work in. If you're not too sure at this stage, then look at evening courses or part time courses in your local community as a taster to something bigger. The internet is a fantastic resource for exploring different subjects and doing small courses that don't require months of commitment or expense, and you may be surprised that something will just click with you and may open the way for further study in that area. This may be a great starting point for you as you won't need to leave your home especially if you have a new baby and another small child. If you have some extra time, you could look at volunteering in a possible field you would be interested in.

Having small children is a lot of work and very time consuming, but you will need to try and find half an hour or an hour a day for you to do something just for you and keep doing it. It will be important for your children as they get older to see that you are important and need to have time for you and to see that you are a person, , with interests and goals.

So, take a bit of time, have a think and explore your options. Keep it in your mind and try and plan out a route, timeline that you would like

Being A Parent

to achieve some of your goals in but be realistic and don't be hard on yourself if it goes a bit stray. If you are focused and really want this, you will achieve everything, and by the time you are 30, you will look back and see how much you have accomplished in a few years.

COVID-19

Q. My 10-year-old daughter has always been slightly reserved and we've always had to really encourage her to take part in her activities and go out with her friends. Once she gets there, she's always fine, but with the break, she seems much more anxious about going back to activities when it's brought up. I think with so much information being spoken about on the radio and tv about COVID-19, she's worried that she'll get it and we will end up sick because of her. How can we get her feeling okay about getting back to normal when we don't know when that will even be?

A. A lot of questions we have been getting recently are around making sure our children are ok as the restrictions are lifted and they go back to some of their normal activities. It's difficult to make sure your children are ok and safe when you're not too sure how you are feeling yourself about the situation, we now find ourselves in due to COVID-19. First thing first is to make sure that you as a parent are ok with life in Covid-19 times. If you are feeling anxious or worried about children going back to activities and eventually school, then they will pick up on this and becomes anxious too. Children may not completely understand what is going on or be able to verbalise it, but they 100% know when something isn't feeling quite right. You may be saying all the right words like "don't worry" or "everything is fine" and then turning away from them and not feeling that way yourself. You may need to take a step back and ask yourself honestly how you are feeling about COVID-19, being safe and the return to normal activities. As there are no definite start dates for activities or school going back at the moment, perhaps you could start to do some of your daughter's activities with her (i.e. soccer, gymnastics) just so she's getting used to doing these activities again, and it won't seem so strange and she may feel more comfortable about going back to the activity. Doing this is just as important as the schoolwork, it's great for her mental wellbeing, her physical health, and to spend some time with you. It doesn't have to be hours and hours, just 20 minutes a couple of times a day will make a huge difference. See if there are videos online of skills that she could try out in the living room or in the garden if the weather is good.

See if any of her clubs are holding Zoom meetings with other team members. She will see some of her friends and how they are getting on with everything. Maybe they could send a message to your daughter letting her know that other members of her teams are looking forward to seeing her. Is she getting any online time with her friends, can she FaceTime any of them for 10 or 20 minutes to see how they are getting on and just have some normal conversations? Could they possibly meet while social distancing, a walk on the beach or play date in the garden? Little by little more and more children are meeting up in estates as it's not possible to keep children indoors all summer and not go out and play. It's really important that our children keep these relationships up and know that for the most part everything is exactly the same, normal life is still happening, but we need to be a bit more careful around hand hygiene and coughing etiquette.

When your daughter's activities do start up again, you need to have a conversation with her about them but reassure her that everything will be fine. Clubs will be making sure that everyone will be safe and that the most important thing is that children get back together to have fun and doing the sports that they love. If she is very anxious and is really struggling, please get in touch and we can talk through some techniques such as Logosynthesis that can help greatly with anxiety. If you are feeling apprehensive and anxious about her going back to activities and meeting with friends, then you need to ask yourself why and what is it in particular that is making you feel this way. Perhaps if you feel you will be anxious about her going to her first class back, ask a friend to take her instead so that she won't be feeding off your anxiety and then be upset.

So, get involved with her activities, see if her clubs are doing any Zoom meet ups, and then see can she facetime some of her school friends. Hope this works out.

Q. My parents have spent a lot of time with my 2 boys since they were born. The lockdown has been really hard on them and my children too. Since the easing of restrictions they have been calling down to our house which has been lovely, but the issue is they want to cuddle the kids (and the kids want to do the same) but I'm saying no as they are both over 70 and I could never live with myself if they contracted COVID-19. How can I have that conversation with both my kids and parents as I don't want to hurt anyone?

A. This is something a lot of parents are experiencing at the moment. It's emotionally difficult to stop your children from hugging their grandparents all of a sudden especially since it's the most natural thing to do and it's something they have done from the very first time they held them. Unfortunately as COVID-19 continues and more and more information is coming out on who it affects the greatest the majority of people who have suffered worst are those over the age of 70 and therefore they are seen as a vulnerable group who need to cocoon and limit their exposure to other people including family. Your parents may be super fit and healthy but this virus acts in a different way and even the healthiest of people have succumbed to it. Your parents perhaps don't care about getting COVID-19 in order to be still able to hug their family and that's understandable but it's very difficult for you to see this possibly happen and for your parents to become unwell. This will only be for a short period of time, and if it means you are going to have to be the bad guy in this situation, then so be it, and they will have to come round to the fact that you are only trying to protect them so they don't become ill, need hospital treatment, and will be around for many more years when all of this has gone away. Let your parents know that your children are now back out doing sports, hanging out with friends a bit more and that you now need to limit their physical contact with them to be safe as you don't know the movements of all the other people your children have been around. Let them know how you wouldn't be able to forgive yourself if your parents became unwell because you allowed them to continue to hug knowing they have been in contact with a lot more people outside of the home. Let them know that you too find the situation so strange and that you want nothing more to have hugs and kisses but you also want your parents to be well and healthy for many years to come and as soon as the restrictions lift they can hug everyone to death! So, just for the time being, no physical contact, but they can have visits and still catch up with the children and you to find out how life is going.

Then you will need to have conversations with your children and use language that is appropriate to their age so as not to go into too much detail that they may not understand. Let them blow kisses or come up with another way of showing their love to their grandparents, you just need to get a little bit creative. You may feel you are being the bad guy but it's ok and you know that it's for the best so wear that badge with honour!!

Q. Since we have been in lockdown, both me and my husband have been around the house a lot more. This has been great at times, we've had some fantastic family times with our 3 children, but at other times it has been extremely stressful. We have really struggled to get a routine going on a regular basis and this means that at different times we have both lost it with the kids and with each other. We have found that there have been moments where we get the kids to bed and are saying barely two words to each other and I'm concerned that this is happening more regularly and that we could be developing some serious martial issues. I don't know what to do, have you any advice?

A. This is like no time any of us have ever experienced, so it is absolutely normal for tensions to be higher. The difficulty in not getting that regular structure going for everyone is that no one knows what the boundaries or parameters are, and this can create extra tension. I would definitely suggest naming it with your husband, and not on the back of an argument. The chances are that you guys are actually fine, it's just this stress is like nothing you have experienced. When we name it, it gets it out in the open and both of you can discuss it. If you feel that talking about it will create an argument, can you write it down in a letter or a notebook? This gives both of you the time and space to digest what the other person is saying and reply, without emotion. The secret is to write from the "I" perspective.

Q. During lockdown, myself and my daughter have been doing a lot of baking. It has been great fun and she has learned so much. She's actually become really confident, which was something that she was lacking. She now wants to bake every day. The issue is that we are all eating these lovely treats every day and we are all putting on weight. We then become quite sluggish and it is a fight to get schoolwork done or exercise. I feel we are now at the time that we need to start getting a bit of normality back, where there aren't treats every day, but I don't want to knock all that confidence that she has built up. Have you any ideas that might work?

A. It's great that you have seen your daughter's confidence rise, and who knows, maybe she'll be hosting *Bake Off* some day!!

One of the real upsides of the lockdown is that parents have had the time to do things like baking with their children, which to me, is just as important as schoolwork. You're teaching your child life skills.

In terms of getting the balance, you're right, there has to be some semblance of normality, and baking and eating sweet treats every day, just isn't a healthy choice for anyone. I'm wondering, can you make an agreement with your daughter? She can bake sweet treats 2-3 times a week, as long as she has gotten her schoolwork and exercise done each day?

Can you look at getting her involved in cooking healthy dinners? She may not be as interested in this, but again, it is a major life lesson, and again, by doing this, she can earn her baking time.

I would definitely look at there being no sweet treats consumed until after school work, exercise and dinner have been had, so it may be useful to set up a daily or weekly plan around what you are doing together and when baking will fit into this plan. This doesn't have to be a negative, but it is absolutely okay to say to your daughter that baking and eating every day (unless she's selling her wares to others!!) isn't necessarily the healthiest option and that way she learns about balance.

DEALING WITH CONFLICT

Q. My kids, especially my 12-year-old son, seem to have developed the habit of having to get the last word in on any discussion we have. Often these remarks are unnecessary and can quickly increase my frustration levels, escalating a simple request into an argument. Any suggestions on how to stop this growing family trend?

A. Firstly, you need to name the problem, don't try to cover it up or be subtle about it. Sometimes you need to be vocal and say this behaviour is not acceptable. Sit the family down, this includes everyone, and name the problem. Explain the situation, that the behaviour is not right, and that everyone is aware of it. Sometimes it's done on purpose, sometimes it's not, but they are aware of doing it. You may get a shrug of the shoulders or a 'don't know' response. You can let everyone know that this behaviour has to stop from now on, and also to let them know that there will be consequences if it continues.

They will test it and see if you remember the consequences or if they can get away with it. It may not be the first time the same scenario plays out, but it could be the second or third time. Make sure you follow through with the consequences. You can give them a warning and remind them of the meeting you had and that the behaviour is not acceptable anymore. This way you are reminding them of the situation and possible consequences, so the decision is in their hands as to how to behave. You will keep calmer as you know you have put consequences in place. With all these things, it has to work in with your family life, especially if it is to be effective. Look at how your family day to day life is and try and find where and when this works best so you can get a good routine going regarding behaviour and consequences.

Q. How do you stop yourself from killing your kids or stop them from killing each other when you are stuck in the house because of the weather?!!

A. First off, don't kill your kids or let them kill each other!!! Pretty difficult to explain to the local gardai or police.

When you are stuck in the house due to snow or bad weather, you always have this romantic idea that everyone will sit around playing board games and bond as a family. This usually lasts all of five minutes and reality comes back as the fighting starts over rules of the game or the cheating that's going on. Others may not want to join in on the family bonding, and this, too, can cause upset. We all need our space and time alone especially when we have been forced into spending time together due to circumstances out of our control.

Try and make a space for each person in the house that is theirs to go to when they need a break and time to themselves especially if it looks as if the patience has run out for that person. It's amazing how quickly they'll come back together knowing that they have a quiet place to go to if needed.

It's a difficult situation sometimes, but, fingers crossed, the snow will melt, and you can kick them off to school again. But Big Tip No. 1, don't kill your kids!!!

Q. Our parents mind our children a couple of days a week while we are at work. We are really trying to stick to a healthy diet during the week, with treats for the weekend or special occasions. We are aware that our parents are treating our kids when they are with them with chocolate, sweets, cakes. We don't want to argue with our parents over the treats or expect our children to say 'no' to their grandparents, but we feel that it's a problem every time they are with them. We know it would not be an issue if they only looked after them occasionally, but we are concerned for our children's long-term health. Any tips on how we can get this across to our parents without taking the joy of grandparenting away from them?

A. So many parents rely on grandparents to mind the kids as both parents are working and bills need to be paid, so it's not an option for one parent to be at home. If you have parents who are able and willing to take on the childcare you are very lucky, and it helps to build a good bond between themselves and their grandchildren. It's a different dynamic; grandparents have raised their own children and there aren't the same responsibilities for them when it comes to looking after their grandchildren. It is a very difficult conversation to have but one that needs to be had. You need to take control of the situation.

Your parents may be doing this wonderful thing for you by minding your children, but they are your kids and not your parents'. It's ok for you to let them know that your children can't have treats every day. If they go to your parents once a week or once a fortnight that's different and treats would be allowed. If they are looking after them 3 or more days a week, you need to let them know that a treat is once a week or at the weekends and not every day. Your parents will be handing you back your children full of sweets and sugar and about to have a sugar crash just as you are trying to get them settled and ready for bed. You are the one that will have to deal with the tears and tantrums when you should be getting an hour of quality quiet time with your children after working all day.

It's important to have the conversation, if it was someone outside of your family looking after your children, you would have the conversation about diet and treats. Just because it's your parents, it's no different—you still want your children to have a healthy diet. If a grandparent is unwilling to stop giving treats all the time, you may need to rethink who is taking care of your children. This may seem a bit extreme, but it is your children's health that matters most, and most grandparents will understand this.

Q. My 11-year-old daughter is refusing to shower and take care of her personal hygiene. She is sporty, and as she is getting closer to being a hormonal teenager, her body odour is more apparent. We have arguments nearly every day about washing herself and it's getting draining. Any advice?

A. This is tough. We have so many things to deal with every day and this shouldn't be a big deal, but it can be. I'm sure you've had a discussion with your child about puberty and how bodies change as we get older and we sweat more when exercising. This is another instance when consequences will need to be put in place. It sounds tough, but it's another part of growing up and an important one, too.

It might be late when she gets home from an activity, so it might not be possible for her to have a shower before bed. If that is the case, the deal is that she has one in the morning, and if there is an argument about it, a consequence is then put in place. At 11 she probably has a favourite device or programme on tv that she couldn't live without. If she decides to argue with you about the showers you can reduce her time on a device or not allow her to watch her programme that evening.

Another consequence could be making her go to bed 30 minutes earlier. Don't work on days for the consequences, work on minutes and gradually increase the time if she continues to argue with you. If you implement days without a device or no tv she will drive you mad within a couple of days and you will give in or your daughter will say she will wash more regularly and before you know it you are back arguing with her to wash. You then have to implement the consequences again and introduce the ban again. Your daughter will quickly learn that if she can live with the consequence for a day or so and continue to annoy you, you will cave in and she'll get what she wants but the situation will not have been resolved. Introduce the consequences as minutes and be consistent about it.

Q. My sons, aged 10 and 8, are constantly fighting and it's driving me crazy. What can I do to sort them out and get harmony in the house?

A. Brothers' fights! They've been doing it for years and they'll keep doing it. Even myself and my own brother had our fair share of ding dongs over the years, it's a natural part of growing up and brothers will annoy each other. There are times when they are not going to be all lovey dovey with each other or even tolerate each other and that's when brotherly fights happen. Unfortunately, you are having to listen to it and deal with the consequences.

I'm sure you wonder what was the point of bringing them up to behave in a certain manner and the time put in to teaching them about respect. A lot of it will be how you deal with this yourself from the start. You may need to take a step back and observe the situation and then see if it's something you need to get involved with or if it will fizzle out naturally and painlessly. How many times have parents become involved with siblings fighting and then become so annoyed and frustrated although there probably wasn't any need to, and five minutes later the children are off playing happily together as if nothing happened!

If the fighting is a bit more serious and you need to step in, try and see what the fight is about and get an idea of how to deal with it and who may be at fault before putting the blame on either child.

You can always introduce boundaries and consequences as a form of trying to discourage the behaviour, but it needs to be consistent and done repeatedly for a proper, long-term result. If you don't stick to it, your children will not have any belief that you will carry it out and therefore will continue as they like. The boundaries you put in place in terms of the children's fighting will be pushed by one or both and that's when the consequences need to really have an impact on them. It could be losing a certain amount of time on the TV or device or an earlier bedtime. Start small and practical, there is no point in banning things for days or weeks as this doesn't work. Start with perhaps 15 minutes less on a device or watching TV or 15 minutes earlier to bed. If your children continue to break boundaries, increase the time by 5 minutes. Eventually they will realise it's not worth losing all the time on things they love doing most.

Q. A couple months ago my almost-9-year-old daughter had her first major disagreement with a friend. She wouldn't really tell us what it was about, only that her friend made her mad and they weren't friends anymore. It has come to our attention since then that our daughter might have a hard time expressing when she's mad.

I think because our oldest son has some anger issues related to autism spectrum disorders, she doesn't feel that it's ok to be angry or mad. How can we guide her to express these emotions appropriately?

A. A lot of people will find with themselves that they went through a time when they couldn't express their emotions. Anger, a lot of the time, is an emotion that is, in fact, masking over another emotion such as sadness, insecurity. It's easier for us to get angry than deal with the other emotions. It's not unusual for a child to experience this.

Our children learn so much from their parents whether we are aware of it or not, and the best way for your child to learn how to express her emotions is to see it in practice through you, her parents. Help them to deal with what is going on by sitting down with them and chatting through it. They may not be able to verbalise exactly what is happening, but they may describe it as a feeling in their stomach or their head. Talk through these feelings and run through a similar scenario with them and how best for them to deal with it.

Perhaps give your child a notebook and allow them to write down words, draw pictures that help them explain what is going on or what has happened in the day. You will see what is going on in their day and you can write back and let them know what is going on in your day, too. It allows your child to process the day without having to use words, and they may see that the day was more positive than they realised.

Try to recognise the emotion they are experiencing. Go through the event and then do some role playing to see how your child could deal with the situation differently. Friends will fall in and out with each other week in and week out. There are always two sides to each story, and emotions can be running high. Sometimes the situation may need to you step in, but usually these things work themselves out in a day or two and your daughter and her friend will have forgotten about what happened. In the meantime, if you step in too early, it will only be you who ends up stressed from the whole situation.

Q. I have three sons and as they're getting older, I'm noticing that my mother is being really negative towards the boys. When we are in her house, she's constantly on at them for nothing in particular. It's now getting to the stage where they don't want to go visit her. I need her to look after them every so often as I work part time, but it's stressing me so much that I'm even considering quitting work. How do I get her to ease up on them?

A. Every few weeks we get a couple of questions about how to deal with grandparents and children, or we get them from grandparents asking how to deal with a certain situation. This can be a hard subject to bring up with your mum. She is a parent and brought you up and possibly other siblings. Your children are not her children and it's about getting a balance and being respectful of each other. Three boys to deal with can be pretty full on as they can be boisterous and noisy. You need to have a conversation with your mum— it's going to be tough. You need to discuss the boundaries you have in place in your home in terms of the boys and ask her what boundaries she would like to put in place when she is looking after them. You need to find a balance that works for everyone.

If you are relying on a grandparent to look after your children, you need to find out the boundaries in their home and you let them know about yours and then agree on something in the middle that will work. You need to have a frank discussion with her. She needs to be able to tell you exactly what it is that is frustrating her. She may be tired; she may feel that she has raised her children and doesn't want to look after the

Dealing with Conflict

grandchildren but hasn't said it because she is aware of you needing a minder. She may just want to enjoy the fun stuff with her grandchildren and not have to discipline them and that's normal. You don't want the relationship between your mum and sons getting to the point where they don't want to see granny outside of the minding times and vice versa with your mum.

After you've done all this, if your mum is still being negative towards your children, you need to look at alternative arrangements and let your mum know that they are your children and your responsibility, and you will take care of it. If you feel they are being disrespectful towards their Granny, you need to deal with that situation. If you feel she is being disrespectful towards your children, you will need to ask her why but do it away from the children, so they are not aware of the conversation. If it's something she can't get over, you will need to sort out alternative childcare.

Q. Our son has moved home after finishing college and has got his first job. We're all finding it tough at the moment as he keeps telling us that we can't tell him what time to be home, as he's an adult, but he still expects his dinner and laundry done for him. How do we get the balance that works for everyone?

A. It's really important that we, as parents, start looking at our older children as young adults and realise that we don't have as much say over their lives now that they have semi moved out to go to college. Saying that, they must still respect you and your home if they are going to stay there over the summer months. There are some parents who will quite happily continue with the cooking and washing for their child as it's only one more body, so what does it matter, but really, they should be contributing to the workload in the home.

If they are working and trying to save for something in particular then it may not be possible to get them to financially contribute while they are living at home, but they can definitely help around the house. If they can give you some money, great, and if you don't really need it you could put it aside for them for the end of the summer. They should be doing their own laundry or offering to do some the housework and offer to cook once or twice a week. Getting them to do this will make them more aware of all the work that goes into keeping a home and will also give them life skills for the permanent move out of the house.

If they are coming in late on a number of occasions and disrupting the house, especially if you have to get up early the next morning, then they need to be made aware of how their behaviour is impacting on the rest of the house. You need to speak to them as an adult, get their input. Treat them as an adult and allow them to contribute, too.

Q. My mother-in-law is constantly calling round to our house. She lets herself in, constantly corrects me in front of my children, gives them treats when I say no, and generally makes me feel like a bad mother and wife. My husband buries his head in the sand and says there's nothing he can do about it. It's putting a real strain on our marriage. Have you any advice on how to make things work?

A. I'm sure there are a lot of people who have experienced this with their in-laws. We want our extended family members to have access with our children and feel welcome in our homes, but it's something that also needs boundaries. This is your home and you didn't marry your partner's family, you married him. You need to find the balance. It's difficult and needs a lot of diplomacy. You will need to sit down with your husband and say that together, as a couple, you need to deal with the way in which your mother in law treats you. It's not right for her to undermine you in front of your children, and you will need to discuss with your husband the behaviour that you are able to tolerate. Can you cope with the fact that she lets herself into your home? If that's not ok, then you need to take away her key or make sure she lets you know that she is calling around. In my opinion, this is just common respect. We all have days when we don't want to see anyone or have to deal with family and that is perfectly acceptable in the privacy of your own home, it is not her place to invade unannounced.

The bigger issue here to deal with first is the way in which she undermines you in front of your children. Granny can sometimes be seen as the higher power, but not in front of you and your children when something needs to be corrected. Grandparents are a great back up in parenting terms. Children have a lot more respect for them and are more likely to listen to them than you, but this needs to be done at the right time and not to undermine you and how you parent your children. Their advice should be as a backup to your parenting and so that your children know you are all on the same page.

Relationships between children and grandparents are so important and your children are lucky to have them in their lives, so you don't want to lose this for you or your children, but grandparents need to be on the same page as you and respect how you have decided to bring up your children. They are, of course, there for fun stuff, too, and treats that parents wouldn't do, so you need to make sure the fun element is allowed.

You need to sit down with your husband and tell him how you are feeling and how his mum's behaviour is making you feel and affecting you emotionally. He may want to bury his head in the sand, but you are his wife and your voice and feelings matter. He has to take some responsibility for his mum's actions and talk to her about what she is doing. She may not even be aware of the impact her actions are having on you, so it needs to be said in as sensitive a way as possible so as not to upset her or turn her against you and make the situation even harder.

If this doesn't work, then this will lead to a more extreme restriction on your mother-in-law's visiting of the home and the children. If she is unable to respect you, your home, and your parenting skills, then she will need to know that she is not welcome until she can see what it is you are trying to achieve for everyone. It's a really tough situation. Life is busy enough, and we should all be trying to help each other out, not cause more hassle and hurt to each other. In-laws can be great most of the time, but every now and again they need to be shown how to respect your relationship and realise that their child is not theirs to interfere with and control any longer.

If you take this on with a hope of a positive outcome, the likelihood is that this is what will happen.

EDUCATION & EXAMS

Q. My daughter is sitting her Junior Cert this year and is becoming increasingly anxious about the exams in June. We have tried to explain to her that although they are important exams, they are not everything. We are afraid she will make herself ill and will become more stressed. Have you any advice on how we can help her get through this and perhaps develop this in preparation for the Leaving Cert?

A. Stress and anxiety in children around exam time is something I'm seeing more and more of and have had an increase in referrals from parents who are worried about their children. It's important that we have the conversation with our children about the exams, and, in the big scheme of things, how they fit in. It's not to take away from how they feel about what they would like to achieve, but to let them know that you don't want them under a lot of pressure or being stressed over exams. Sometimes schools can put a lot of pressure on children to achieve top results and this doesn't help. Anxiety and worry in children can be difficult to deal with. We may tell our children not to worry about exams, study, but they are going to do it anyway. Anxiety is an emotion about the future, when we worry about the worst possible outcome to a situation and we rarely think about the best possible outcome. More than likely the best possible outcome is what will happen, but it's difficult for them to see this.

To help your child, it would be good to try some calming techniques or mindfulness, make sure they are getting enough sleep, exercise, and are eating right. It's important also during the exams that every evening they have a bit of down time, i.e. going to the movies with friends, keep training in their sports. Help them create a good study plan that gives them good break times in their study time. Children learn to study in many different ways, one shoe does not fit all. It may be worth doing the Multiple Intelligences quiz that can help identify how your child learns best, this may include having music playing in the background as they work or having key points around their room on post it notes. There should be 40 minutes max of study and then have a break and have a cut-off point early in the afternoon. Leave the evening for socialising with friends and just let them chill out.

Help them to get organised for the next day, prepared well for the exams, and that they get a good night's sleep.

Q. We recently got feedback during parent teacher conferences that our 8-year-old daughter is struggling with speaking up in class. She will only raise her hand to answer a question if she is certain she knows the right answer—things that are safe, like "What day of the week is it?" When called on for an answer, she freezes. Additionally, she's falling behind in math as she won't ask for help if she doesn't understand an assignment. How can we help her to be more comfortable with speaking up in class and advocating for herself?

A. This can be worrying for some parents. It is understandable why teachers try to encourage all their students to partake in giving presentations or speaking in front of their classmates as it develops confidence and gives them the opportunity to discuss something that is important to them. They will get used to talking in front of other people. Of course, there are those who embarrass easily, are introverts and do not find it easy to speak in front of others. They may find any excuse not to attend school on the day of a presentation or event when they may be expected to speak up in class.

If may be worth talking to your child about how they feel, what it is that makes them worry about speaking in front of other people. It might be a good idea to go through some of the techniques you would use as an adult to get through these situations. Let them know that you have felt this way too and have suffered nervousness, that it is a normal response to the situation. Take the time to spend some time with them and what might help them to get through the presentation or speak in front of their classmates. If there is a worst-case scenario that your child has perhaps work through a possible solution and don't dismiss how they are feeling even if the likelihood of it every happening is very slim.

In regard to the maths class, it may be worth speaking to their teacher and letting them know that your child is afraid to ask a question in class if they don't understand the problem. The teacher may decide to check in with your child during the class to see how they are getting on and may encourage them gently to speak in class. If everyone is on the same page, then you can all work together to help your child's confidence and ultimately help them to grow and develop their skills.

Q. My daughter is 9 and is getting into a lot of trouble in school. When the school contacts us about any issues, we sit down with her and explain that she can't behave this way. My wife and I are not confrontational people, but we are really worried that the school might be picking on our child. How can we approach the whole situation with the school as we don't want her being expelled?

A. You definitely don't want this situation to escalate to the point where your daughter is being expelled, so intervention of some type would be good. In order for your daughter to be expelled from school there would have to been certain disciplinary steps taken by the school to get to that stage.

There could be a few things going on here. Your child may be behaving this way as a call for help, although it seems a bit strange, and there could be something going on. Your child could be sitting in class and not understanding what the teacher is teaching and it's easier to get put out of the class or misbehave than to put your hand up and admit that you don't understand the subject. It could be that they can't see the board properly and are lost as they can't follow the lesson. This may take a little bit of time to explore every aspect of your child's school day but will be worth it.

As for the misbehaving in school, this needs to be addressed and there needs to be consequences. It's good to see that you have sat down and discussed this with your daughter, but if she is continuing to behave in this manner then stricter boundaries and consequences may need to be used. You say you are not confrontational people and that's great, but sometimes when it comes to our children, they need to see that you are in control and sometimes you need to put your foot down. You can be respectful with your children, but as a parent you need to give them boundaries to keep them safe, and then consequences if they break these boundaries so they learn where the dangers are or where their behaviour is not acceptable.

These boundaries change and get bigger as your child grows and learns to become more responsible for themselves. You may need to introduce tougher consequences so if and when your daughter chooses to misbehave in school it may be enough of a consequence for them to think about their actions before they carry them out.

There could be a personality clash between your daughter and her teacher, and she may well feel that she is being picked on by the teacher. You will need to explore this further. Have a meeting with the teacher and try to get a better idea of what is going on. Approaching the school in a calm manner and with an attitude that you want to fix this situation will help immensely. You're not going in accepting that your child is bold and it's all their fault, but you will be going in with the mind of looking at both sides of the story and being open to the best solution possible.

Let the school know that there are boundaries and consequences at home in relation to how your daughter is behaving in school and that you are aware of it. More open conversations between you and the school may lead to the root of the problem a lot quicker too.

It will take a bit of work, but your daughter's wellbeing and her experience in school is really important, so having a good relationship with the school would be a good idea and try to solve the issues in the best way possible.

Q. My 17-year-old is obsessed with the fact that exams are coming and feels like "your life depends on them... " How do I help her to relax into it and realise that while it is serious, it's not life threatening?

A. There will be parents listening to this and wishing their children were so focused as they struggle to get them to pick up a book! There will be other parents who can relate to this listener's dilemma and be worried for their own children, too. Some children can put so much pressure on themselves to achieve and it can also be coming from teachers and parents especially if they are a child that has always had good results and has worked hard.

This pressure seems to be coming from your daughter on to herself and she feels the need to get the best results possible. She feels the need to spend every waking hour studying so she is certain she has covered every possible topic that may come up and all other aspects of her life have fallen away.

If you can help your daughter set up a study plan this will give her a more realistic day that will include study, sleep, time off, sports, family time. If she is in full-time education and exams are approaching, then each of her classes will be study based, all geared towards the exams, so this is a large chunk of study your daughter is doing every day but she is possibly not seeing it like that. She will need to take this study into account when she is planning out her afternoon/evening study.

Try to set up study blocks of no more than 40 minutes as after this time our brains don't process the information the same way, especially teenage brains, and without knowing it, we have switched off, become distracted, and are becoming tired. After the 40 minutes, make sure your daughter is getting away from her desk, stretching out her legs and taking a 10 – 15 minute break. Make sure she is drinking water and having healthy snacks at this time. In the evening your daughter needs to concentrate on only 2-3 subjects max, and on some evenings less as it's important to have evenings off, too, where you spend time with friends, family or take part in your sports. This down time is so important as it helps you to relax, helps your brain to process all the studying, and gives you a break.

No one can constantly work under pressure, whether it's external or internal. This needs to be explained to your daughter, and there will need to be a compromise when it comes to the amount of time your child would like to study.

It is very difficult to explain to your child that the exams aren't everything, when nearly everyone else around her is telling her how important they are. We all know successful people who left school early and now have very accomplished working lives. They may have decided to study later in life after working for so many years. You will know people who failed exams the first or even second time but now have good jobs and enjoy what they are doing. There are so many alternative ways to achieve the profession you want outside of the normal school, college, route. Try to have these conversations with your daughter, she may not be interested but at least if you have talked to her about it she has heard it and can process it when she feels ready.

As long as your daughter knows you are there for her and are proud of her no matter what she achieves, this, too, may help her to break away from the study a bit more and get more of a balance. Best of luck.

Q. My son does not care about his state exams. He refuses to study and says the education system is a joke. I'm fit to murder him. What can I do to encourage him?

A. This is the case for so many parents especially around exam time. The traditional education system we have in this country does not work for the majority of students. It doesn't help them to explore possible future professions or look at further education that may be of interest to them. The state exams here work best for people who are able to learn off and retain information and then spit it all out again when it comes to the exams. It is very difficult for the majority of students to learn like this, and it can be a very stressful time for them as they try to learn and retain as much information as possible for the exams.

Our education system can be very rigid, and it may not be the best learning environment for your child; we all have different ways of learning. If you would like to explore what type of learner your child may be drop me an e-mail and we can look at it.

If you are really struggling with your son and his study, you may need to just go through it and let him sit the exams. You can keep encouraging him to study but not nag as this will lead to arguments. If it is causing upset in the house for everyone it's not worth fighting about. Have the conversation with him about what he would like to do after he finishes school, what are his interests, and see if there are alternative courses he can do outside of the college/university route. You need to let him know that he will be expected to further his education after school, and if he's not interested in this then he will need to find employment and contribute to the family household.

After you have laid all this information on him he may be more willing to give the study another go, and if not, all you can do is support him as best you can during the exams and be there when the results come out regardless of the outcome. He may be devasted if he fails his exams and wish he worked harder. He may decide to repeat his exams, which may give him more time to decide on the next step in his life.

Q. My parents are putting so much pressure on me 'cause they want me to go into the medical profession. I would love to be a teacher, but my parents have said they won't support me, so I have no choice. How can I get them to realise that I need to follow my heart?

A. I have had parents in the past sending their children to me to get me to motivate them to study more or to see things from their perspective in terms of third-level choices, but that's not how it works. I'm not another voice for the parents to try and get their children to do something they don't necessarily want to do. I have to come from the child's perspective. Some parents need to be aware that the path your child takes may not be the one you would have chosen for them. If you put yourself in your child's position would you have wanted someone telling you what profession you had to pick even if it wasn't something you were interested in? There will be loads of parents disagreeing with this, that they have good jobs, wages and security because our parents made us take a certain career path.

We need to remember that we only have one life, this doesn't mean we need to be reckless with our lives and choices but your working life can be long and it needs to be something that you enjoy doing, that keeps you motivated and gets you up and about every day.

You need to encourage your child in their chosen profession, the chances are it will change a couple of times before they find the job they are passionate about. Our circumstances change so much during our lives and no one can predict the future. The important thing here is that you find a career you are interested in, helps you financially and lets you grow as an adult. We as parents shouldn't put our expectations on our children in terms of their college or career choices.

Perhaps you can sit down with your parents and let them know that you have heard them and taken their side into consideration, but your choice for a career is teaching and you will pursue it. It may be difficult to source finances if your parents are not willing to help, but it is possible especially if it is what you would really love to do as your career.

I'm sure there are parents screaming at me now that this shouldn't happen, that children should not be allowed to make such big decisions on their own and go their own way, but why not? It's not your life, your decision. You have a life whether you are happy in it or not but it's not your child's and it's not your right to decide their future. You are needed to help and support them, offer advice and be there when it gets tough and they need some help. Most of the time our advice to our children is good and it's been learnt through our own mistakes, but we all need to make the mistakes and learn from them.

Your future may seem a bit uncertain especially as your parents are not in support of you and you may have some really hard and tough times ahead of you. All families go through their up and downs. Hopefully your parents will listen to you and understand your decisions. If not, I'm sure there will be other people who can help you out, support you in your career and your parents will eventually come around.

 My child is always listening to music when she studies, but there's no way she's studying. She says it helps but we always end up in an argu-

Education & Exams

ment. What is the best way to study in your opinion?

A. Everyone has a certain way of studying and taking in information. There are 9 different intelligences and each of these has a different way of learning and absorbing information. When we were younger, we were made to go to our room, no distractions, and stay up there for hours studying. None of us did that, we all got distracted and possibly did every other thing but study.

You may need to figure out with your child the best way for them to study and put a study plan in place. If your child is studying while listening to music then doing well in their exams, or completing their homework, on time and to a good level, then they know what helps them to study better and you need to give them the benefit of the doubt. The proof is always in the pudding, and if it turns out to be the opposite, then you need to have a conversation with them about how they study and look at another way of tackling it.

It may not be the ideal way for you to learn or study, but that doesn't mean it's not working for your child. There is a guide to the 9 intelligences that I can run through with you to get some insight into the different ways of studying.

Of course, if the music is blaring out of the room and disrupting the whole house you may need to have a chat.

The bigger picture is to help your child, help her to keep calm while studying, and hopefully to keep calm when going into exams.

Q. My son just did his leaving certificate. By his own admission he didn't do any work at all for it. He kept telling us he was on top of things, but last night he came to me really upset saying he did nothing and he really worried that he will fail and doesn't want to go back to repeat as he hates school. What can I do to help him?

A. Sometimes in life our children need to learn about natural consequences, so what does this mean? As parents raising children, we put in place boundaries, rules, how to live in society as you can't just go out and do what you want, when you want. All of these things are done to keep our children safe and help them to learn about life and give them the tools to take on their own lives when they leave you as young adults. Putting consequences in place come in when our children over-step the boundaries, which they will do naturally to see how safe they are, and to check that you will push back and stop them from doing something silly or harmful to themselves or others. We don't always consider natural consequences for our children as we are usually trying to stop them ourselves instead of letting the inevitable happen and seeing how they learn from the experience. Of course, we're not talking about dangerous situations for our children, especially anything that could physically harm them. Sometimes the results of letting them learn through natural consequences can have a longer lasting impact on our children then us telling them no or trying to give them advice to keep them safe.

For example, if one of my children go outside and take another child's ball without asking, they may get a shove or shouted at, or something taken from them, and this is a natural consequence. There is a natural response from something they have done, and because it is a peer who has given out, they will remember this and it will stay with them. They may think twice before they do it again. As a parent you don't step in; your child may come to you to let you know they have been shoved, and your natural instinct is to jump in and help them, but in reality that is of no benefit as the situation will only be intensified and could lead to even more problems for your child. What you might discover is that your child did take the ball and then it's an opportunity to have a talk with your child about their actions and the consequences of behaving in this manner.

In this instance, and it's a really tough one, you may need to let your child sit with the feelings of not having done enough for their exams. He will have to deal with it, acknowledge the feelings, and learn to live with this uncertainty until his results come out a couple of months later. In reality maybe your son won't have done as badly as he thinks and may get a college offer so he can move on. On the other hand, he may fail or not get the points he needs. This may be as a result of not knowing what he wants to do in college or the rest of his life and this may give him the opportunity to reflect on what it is he wants to do next. He may figure this out himself, not have his hand held, and the decisions made for him or sorted out by his parents. This is the natural consequences to his decision not to study more for his exams and that is life. If we wrap our kids up in a bubble, life is going to be really tough for them when they do become adults and are facing the world on their own. They won't have someone fixing everything for them, making sure they are ok all the time.

This is not to say that you pull all support from your child and leave them completely on their own to figure this problem out. You will need to sit and talk to your son about what he thinks are possible options if the results do not go his way instead of you coming up with the options and forcing one on him. This will only annoy them as they are well aware of the situation they have put themselves in and need encouragement at this point and a more adult approach to fix it.

It will be up to your son to do some research on courses that he could do instead of having to go back and repeat his exams. It's a very difficult situation to be in to try and take a step back and allow your son to come up with decisions about his future now, especially as we can still see them as being children and we feel we should always protect them.

If your son hates school, the issue of going back to repeat his exams will need a lot of discussion. Will he work any harder if he's not enjoying it or hating going to school every day? Maybe he needs to go and get a job or a course that has nothing to do with what he would like to study. This will be a reality check for him as he is the one who didn't do the work, he didn't study so he needs to find the solution, and staying at home and doing nothing is not the solution. He might, or you might, blame the school or teachers who didn't help, and this may be an element to the lack of study, but he is the one who admitted that he didn't do any work for the exams. He needs to take responsibility, needs to deal with the situation that is out of his control, and come up with some options that he can then sit down and discuss with you and you can then help him to get this up and running, but it's up to him to do most of the work and not let him sit around and expect you to do it. This will only teach your child that you will always rescue them and they won't learn how to deal with real life situations when they are grown adults. This type of behaviour towards your children doesn't empower them and can lead to you still having a 28- year-old son living at home with you who has no social life, no job, no future. You will still be doing all their housework, cooking, and they will have no respect for you.

So, let your son get through the exams, help him to study before each exam as best he can. Create a calm atmosphere for him during this time and then let him blow off some steam for a couple of days after or maybe just sleep. Then comes the time to sit and discuss the future and what he feels will happen in August. It will all work out, just maybe not in the way you had planned for your child.

Q. My daughter has taken a year out after her exams last year and has worked for most of the year in a local bar. This has been good for her as she's got some independence and learned a bit about life. I'm a bit worried about her not going to college and just staying working. How can I help her realise that she should get her education done now, which will improve her chances of a decent career?

A. We put a huge amount of weight behind the importance of going to college and getting a degree. If your daughter wanted a break studying and wanted to work and get some money for herself, then that's great and she has been working the whole year, which showed her commitment to the job and what she wished to do for the year.

Parents become worried about their children getting comfortable in this type of environment as their child is earning, still living at home, and has a nice lifestyle as a result. Money is a huge draw for a lot of young people, and having it can be a pull in the direction of staying employed and perhaps not going to college. It's important to take a step back and not push her too much in terms of her future plans if she is working, contributing to the household. Her work in the bar may start out at pulling pints, but could lead to management, which is another way of learning just on a practical basis and is worth more to future employers as she has gained valuable experience from the bottom up. She may then decide to study part time or in the evenings to further her education while still working.

If you choose to push your daughter into full-time education, she may hate it and drop out in the first 3 months, which will have been a waste of money for you and will have been stressful for both you and your child. Some parents will feel that kids just have to do what they are told, go to college, get the degree, and then find a job whether or not it's something they want to do. This may work for some children, and they may be glad in the long run that their parents pushed them in a certain direction, but there are also children who will feel that they never got the chance to pursue a career they were interested in and that's not what you want for your child.

You know your child best and if you feel she needs encouragement to go to college, then give it to her, help her to make the decision, and support her. If she chooses not to do this and decides to keep working, then a different set of rules will need to be implemented in the family home if she continues to live there. This might include paying rent, contributing towards bills and other household expenses. It will be a great life lesson for your daughter. If, in a couple of years' time she decides to turn around and accuse you of keeping her from going to college, you can have a simple conversation with her and jog her memory as to the decision she choose to make. She will need to take responsibility for the decision she made and that you supported her just like you would have supported her if she went to college.

So the next step is to go out for dinner or a cuppa with your daughter and discuss what her plans are for the future. Let her know how proud you are of her for working and supporting herself for the last year and that you will continue to support her into the future. Get her to think about what she may like to study; you may be surprised as she may already have planned it all out but hasn't included you yet! Maybe she won't know what she would like to do, so this may be an opportunity to go through some options, not necessarily full-time education, but perhaps part time or evening that she may be interested in. There are so many other options out there in terms of studying and working at the same time. Your daughter is young and has loads of time to do both if that is what she would like to do. Best of luck.

Q. Once the kids are back in school, how long should you give them to settle back into "school mode?"

A. This may seem like a non-issue to some parents, but making sure you get back into a school routine as early as possible in September can make or break the rest of the year for you and your children.

It's not a case of how long you should give them as every child is different and some will get back into the school routine straight off, but for others it may take a few weeks. Allow the first week or two to be as stress free as possible by setting up a routine and sticking to it, but at the same time not being overly frustrated if it doesn't work every morning. This can especially be the case if you have a child who is going from primary to secondary school and there may be an earlier start and more to organise. If, after a couple of weeks, there is still a battle to get them up and out, then you may need to sit down with them and have a chat about how important it is that everyone is doing their bit to help with the morning routine. Ask them what it is they need to get back on track, let them know that you are trying to support them, set them up for a good day, and you are not trying to nag them about getting up and going to school.

Teachers in school will be hitting the ground running with homework and projects, so they will need the routine as soon as possible.

You don't want things to carry on too long as you will become frustrated and tired as the afterschool activities start back, too, and you will have a full day of running around after your children. Try not to get too stressed if this goes on longer than necessary. You can't force your kids to do anything, but you can let them know that you are there to help them in a positive way.

Making sure that they have everything packed the evening before can make the mornings a lot easier. Have lunches made the night before so they are just ready to pack. Having these couple of small things done the day before can make for a much more smooth-running morning especially if you are running late.

Let your children know that you don't want to be shouting and giving out to them in the mornings, and that you are asking very little of them to make sure the home is happy and smooth running for them before they go to school.

Once you have the morning routine going well you can start to look at the homework, study routine, especially if you have a child who is in a year that has state exams at the end.

Q. Me and my wife are at loggerheads when it comes to our eldest son. He is going into secondary school and he has always been very artistic. This is great and is something we really encourage, but I feel that when it comes to his subject choices in school, that he should be taking classes that will give him the best chance to get a good job when he leaves, while my wife says we should let him choose what he loves. Obviously, he agrees with my wife. Any advice on how we can find a common ground?

A. You need to find a common ground that works for everyone. It is very difficult for a young teenager to know what subjects may or may not appeal to them in secondary, or may be of benefit to them in the long term, as they probably have no idea what they would like to do when they go to college or get a job. Some schools may offer taster classes in all the subjects that are on offer, and this may give your son a better idea for final choices. There could be something that jumps right out at him that he never thought he would be interested in.

With your partner, you need to sit down and look at your son's strengths. If he is very good at art, then perhaps he should do it as a subject. There is also technical drawing and other art-based subjects that he may be interested in and lead on to a field he may like to pursue in college. Doing subjects he is interested in can make the secondary school experience much more enjoyable and he is more likely to work hard on these subjects and do well in them. Let him pick the subjects he would like to do.

We all change, our tastes change, and society has changed. Most people now going on to college change their course or go on to study something very different, and then may go into a very different field when it comes to work. It is very rare now that you have a child who knows from very young what they would like to do and end up doing that in adult life. Children have so many more options open to them, and as long as they work hard and commit to something, they are most likely going to achieve their goals. Life is long with loads of turns along the way. Our job as parents is to equip our children with life lessons to help them on their way, whatever that may be, and for them to know that we will always be there for them to support and encourage.

Q. My 18-year-old is getting his leaving certificate results today and he hasn't been able to sleep for the last few nights. I've tried to tell him that he'll be fine, but he's a nervous wreck. I'm now worrying that he hasn't done as well as he hoped and am a bit lost in how to make him okay. Any advice?

A. You can't fix your child, unfortunately. We would love to be able to make everything ok for them, and make this journey as smooth as possible, but that's not the reality of life or a way in which your son will learn about life.

Take the pressure off yourself trying to fix your son. We regularly discuss on this podcast how important it is to build resilience in our children and show them how they can do this by overcoming setbacks themselves. He may do really well and get the course he wants, or get a second or third round offer, or may not get want he wants at all, and you will need to look at the next step. Sometimes it's just about being there for him, not judging or telling him he could have done better. He will need time to think about what he would like to do next, and this is when he will need you to help him with that next step.

He may not want your advice or support straight after he gets his results as he tries to deal with it himself, as he may be in a panic about his future. He will want to be left alone to be annoyed and frustrated with himself and that's ok for a day or two. You don't need to have any conversations with him right now about his future or his options, and more than likely after he's blown off a bit of steam, he will come to you with possible solutions or ask for your advice. You can then sit down with him and look at options more clearly and set out a plan for the upcoming academic year. There are so many options for young people now in terms of courses, and not all of them require high grades to get onto them. There are not many young adults who know exactly what they want to do after school for their career, and many adults will have had a number of varying careers before they find one that suits them or they want to work at. This could be a great opportunity for your son to enroll in a post-leaving cert course in a field that he thinks he may like to get into as this will give him a taste of the course and he will not be committing to 3 or 4 years study straight away.

Be there for your son, don't rush into solving the problem and you may just be really surprised with his results!

Q. My school experience was not a pleasant one. I'm worried that with my child getting older, I'll struggle with the homework, and I really don't want to pass on my anxiety around school to my child and see her look at school as something negative. How can I support her and relax a bit when it comes to schoolwork?

A. There are a few things to cover here. Firstly, your experience is your experience, and most likely it won't be the same for your child. School has changed so much over the years. I work a lot with schools and am in and out of them regularly and they are so different. They are much more friendly environments with laughter and fun, and teachers and pupils have much better relationships. Be involved with the school on a voluntary basis, which will help you see it in a different way and be positive with them especially if something does come up. If you approach them with a positive attitude, they are already of that mind, and things will be resolved much quicker and with good results.

If you are doing homework with your child now, the chances are they know what they are doing and will be more than capable of working through it themselves. If something comes up in the future, research it online, the internet has some amazing resources for parents, children, and teachers to help with schoolwork, and most schools are now regularly using online tools in the classroom every day. You and your child can figure it out together. It may take more time, but it will be worth it. It's also ok not to have all the answers for your children and to have to look things up, no one knows everything. If you are struggling with one subject in particular, look into doing a refresher course for parents, the internet has many online courses you could do in the evenings.

Your experience when you were younger was very real for you, and the anxiety around it is understandable and can stay with us for a long time, but try and put it in its place and see that your child is in a really important stage of their life. And it can be really enjoyable for both of you, and you will see your child develop in so many ways by getting involved with them and helping them through the good and bad bits!

GRIEF & LOSS

Q. Our 7-year-old son had a hen that he had raised from an egg in school last year. Unfortunately, the hen was killed by an animal last night and our son is very upset. We are unsure how to deal with his grief, one minute he is fine, then the next he is talking about the hen and crying. Do you have any suggestions on how we can help our child deal with the death of his pet? He knows about heaven, but I don't think he really understands. We told him that he can dream about his chicken at night, but he is still really sad. He has a few feathers from the hen that he carries around and sometimes talks to as if his pet is still alive. Is this normal?

A. The loss of a pet is hard on adults, but for children it is really tough. It can be very overwhelming for them to deal with and sometimes can be their first experience of death. First thing is to let your son know that it's ok to be feeling sad. Sometimes, and especially with boys, they can be made to feel that they have to "man up" and shouldn't be showing their feelings. He needs to know it's ok to cry and be sad about the loss. We become very attached to our pets and they are like a member of the family, so we need to be able to grieve for them.

What you don't want to do is build any false hopes in your child that the pet is going to come back. Your son is going to learn a lot about himself and about the circle of life as he deals with this loss. It is very sad, but it is normal for him to want the hen to still be alive, he is dealing with his grief and this event has only just happened. No one knows how long grief lasts for, it is very much an individual experience. Maybe you could set up a little shrine for the hen using the feathers, somewhere your son can go to if he wants to chat to his pet and maybe in the future you could chat about getting another pet. For now, your son needs to deal with the loss of his much-loved hen and also, he needs to know that you are there for him to help him through the grief.

Grief & Loss

Q.

Friends of ours were broken into while they were away. Lost some jewellery and a few other things. They have 2 young girls aged 9 and 5. Not surprisingly the girls are not sleeping at all well, which adds stress to the family. Thoughts as to what they should do and suggested words of comfort?

A.

First thing so sorry to hear this has happened to you. It's so intrusive into your family life. Some people can become very upset over the loss of property, but worse is the intrusiveness of someone in your home, your safe personal space for your family. For the kids, they are very aware of what happened. It's important to acknowledge what has happened. They are old enough to understand. Don't try and brush over it and pretend it never happened.

They are working from an emotional state when they are trying to go to sleep. Logically you have told them they are safe, and no one will hurt them. That you have an alarm on the house and the break-in happened when you were out of the house. That's the logical side. The not sleeping is an emotional response. Let them know that it's ok to be upset.

Look at their routine and see when a quiet, calm time before bed is that you can discuss how they are feeling. Give them a notebook and let them draw a picture or write down their emotions. Some children find this easier if they don't have the words or can't say it to you. A fairy door in their room might ease their worry, a fairy sent especially to them to keep them safe.

If it's an ongoing issue, you may need to seek professional help. Here at Help Me To Parent, we use a programme called Logosynthesis that helps to release the negative energy that it attached to the emotion. You could look for a local practitioner that could explain the process to you. We have had effective results with the programme for adults and children.

Console your child, let them know it's ok to be upset and that you will get through it together as a family.

Grief & Loss

Q.

My sister passed away from cancer recently and my 10-year-old son was really close to her. He's been so strong the whole way through this tough time for the family, but I'm worried he is bottling up his feelings to protect all of us. Have you any suggestions to get him to open up?

A.

It's a very sad and difficult time for your family, and such a tragic loss of someone so young. You are dealing with your own grief and pain from the loss and now you are concerned about your son and his reaction to the passing of a very close and much-loved aunty. Everyone processes death in a different way, and in turn, everyone grieves in different ways. Some people will be outwardly grieving, regularly crying, or talking about how they are feeling and dealing with the death of a loved one. Others may be less so, may just seem to be grieving at the time of the death and funeral, and then there are those who keep it all in as they may be worried about the other people around them and don't want to add everyone else's pain and sorrow.

Don't try and sit him down and have a face-to-face about how you are feeling and your concerns about his demeanour since your sister passed away. He may well just be figuring it out for himself and dealing with his emotions himself first. He may be trying to figure out how he is going to see his life in the future without his beloved aunt in it. You could bring up the possibility of having a chat with him first and see how he feels about that, but don't push it, let him take the lead and be there for him.

In the meantime, there are things you can do for your son. Perhaps give him a notebook where he can write down how he is feeling, how he is finding his day-to-day life. It may help him to get his thoughts and emotions out of his head and onto paper, which can have a great effect on helping him to process what is going on. If he does this on a daily basis, he will go to the book and write down how he is feeling, especially if something upsets him in school or he is feeling emotional about his aunt's death. If he has been protecting you up to this point, he may find writing in the book a great help as he will feel he can put anything down in it and not have to come to you. The chances are if he doesn't start to get these emotions out in some way, it will build up and he won't be able to contain how he is feeling. If this does happen, let him get it all out as he will feel so much better and then gently approach him with a view to chatting about what he is feeling.

Keep checking in with him, but not routinely, just casually if you are in the car together or when you are out for a walk. You could bring up your sister in the conversation around a memory you had about her and something in particular she liked. It could be related to what you are doing with your son at the time.

Don't put pressure on him to get out his emotions, be there for him and let him grieve in his own way. You will get through this together, but it's going to be a difficult, sad time for a while for all of you. Take care of yourselves.

MANAGING BEHAVIOUR

Q. My son has made a lot of progress over the years, but there is one thing we are struggling with. He refuses to take responsibility for his actions and somehow finds a way to blame others. My husband and I have addressed this many times, but it continues to happen. He has admitted to us it's about wanting to be right. How can we teach him to take responsibility or be accountable for his negative behaviours? It's very frustrating as we want him to learn from his mistakes, but he refuses to admit he was ever wrong.

A. Depending on your son's age, perhaps he needs to be given responsibility for something outside of the home, e.g. small job/contribute to a charity through volunteering. Through this he will need to learn to take responsibility for the tasks he has been given, and he will be answerable to people he does not have a close relationship with if there is something that needs to be corrected or questioned.

The Karpman Drama Triangle can be a good source to see how your son's behaviour is affecting him. There are two triangles, Negative and Positive. The Negative Triangle has a Victim, Persecutor and Rescuer. Your son may feel he is the Victim, everything is happening to him, and he feels "poor me" all the time. He may then go from this to the Persecutor role and can continue to go between these to justify his behaviour towards you and other people.

Life has a great way of teaching people how they should behave towards other people. It may be a case that he walks out of the house one day and someone punches him in the face because of the way he has behaved.

Maybe we need to allow our children to get a metaphorical punch in the face so they can learn the consequences of their actions. We can't always wrap our children in cotton wool, and sometimes the best way to learn is through our mistakes.

Q.

My daughter is constantly saying "sorry" even when she hasn't done anything wrong. What can I do to help her realise that she doesn't need to do this all of the time?

A.

I've noticed this a lot more recently in both children and adults; it's something I also find myself doing. It seems as if it has become an automatic reaction. People apologise for no reason. I think with children it can be an automatic thing to deal with the world around them. In children between 5- and 8-years-of-age, they are starting to notice the world a bit more, and their environment has become a lot bigger, not just the house they live in or the school they go to. They are more aware of events that are going on in the world, and a lot of this can be upsetting and cause insecurity in a child. This can be daunting for some children, they can struggle with it, and an automatic result can be to apologise for things so that a situation doesn't escalate, and they won't get into trouble. It's not a conscious thing, it's a default mechanism to keep a calm environment for them by apologising.

Have a look to see if there is a pattern to your daughter's apologising. It's ok to sit down with her and explain to her that she doesn't need to apologise for everything, especially if it's not something that needs an apology like misspelling a word or forgetting how to do a maths problem.

Maybe come up with another word for sorry, like "ok," "excuse me," or "pardon." Have a conversation about the instances when an apology is necessary. Sometimes children who apologise for everything don't realise when a situation comes up that they should apologise for, and this can be confusing and frustrating for everyone.

If it's not getting better, and your daughter is continuing to apologise for everything, and is becoming more distressed and anxious, it may be worth further investigating what's going on and perhaps seeking the support of a professional counsellor for children.

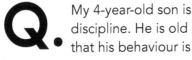

Q.

My 4-year-old son is getting more difficult to discipline. He is old enough to understand that his behaviour is wrong, but we need some

Managing Behaviour

ideas for better discipline for his age.

A.

It's a time when parents struggle. With a 4-year-old, they are probably going to crèche or getting ready to go to primary school. It is a time when children of this age realise there is a much bigger world outside of their usual four walls, and it can be challenging for them. They are not the centre of the universe, and they will start to push boundaries. The boundaries and consequences you had in place up to this point may not work now. They need to change as they grow up and experience new challenges.

We put boundaries in place to keep our children safe and to help them learn of dangers like crossing a busy road, not touching a hot surface. We do it so they can understand the structure of the world they live in. They are going to have to learn a daily routine of getting up, school, homework, bedtime. Unless you are taking your family to a remote forest to raise them yourself, they will need to learn boundaries. For their personal boundaries they need to learn what is ok or not ok for them. As parents, children need to know that you will step in if the boundaries have been overstepped. They may not be able to police themselves and they will need you to do it, although they will push boundaries! This is very useful, especially as we get into teenage years when we are around our children less and may not know what they are doing all the time. You will need to have discussions with your children about naked selfies. You need to build their boundaries, so your child knows it's ok not to get involved in certain types of behaviour if they don't feel comfortable with it. There needs to be consistency with the boundaries and also room to negotiate as your child gets older.

If your 4-year-old's bedtime is 7pm then that's the time they go to bed and stick to it. As they get older, you can change this to a later time as long as they have shown in the past that they can stick to the bedtime routine.

It would be great if our children trusted everything we said to them in terms of events that could be dangerous to them. There will always be children who have to learn through experience. For example: telling your child of the dangers of touching a hot stove and they believe you versus the child who has to touch the stove to believe that you are not lying to them. It may take that child a little longer to understand boundaries and why you have them, and they may need more consequences to keep them safe.

Consequences are important. Children need to know where the line is, where is the step too far, and this is very important going into teenage years. You need to look at the boundaries you have in place now for your 4-year-old and see if they need to change, are they working for you? Do you reduce screen time, take away a favourite toy so the child can see that there are consequences to their behaviour? It is also important to make sure that any parent who is around your child, perhaps helping with childminding, that they are aware of the boundaries and consequences and stick to them. It's not easy, it takes time and dedication, but will benefit your child and you in the long run. It will be trial and error, sometimes it may not work, and you need to start again, but it will help with your child's behaviour for the better.

Q. Our children really want a dog and we are seriously considering it. What steps can we put in place now before the puppy arrives to teach the children about their responsibilities for the care of it? It will be their first pet and we feel they could learn a lot from the experience if we can get the responsibility aspect right without affecting the excitement of having a puppy in the house.

A. A lot will depend on how old your children are. Pre-teens and teens will be able to take on a lot more responsibility and will be more aware of what the dog needs. Younger children may not be able to help as much, but that doesn't mean they can't help out. You can chat about how this puppy is a family pet, not just mum and dad's, and everyone will need to do their bit. Need to explain that this will be a small puppy and not like other dogs they may know or have experience with. It won't be trained like older dogs and may be a bit more jumpy, but will also need a lot of sleep as it is still young. Help them realise what to expect, belongings may get chewed and a new puppy can be nippy. Explain what they can do to help, e.g. don't leave toys down that the dog may chew, take them for little walks and help to clean up any accidents or poo outside. Let them know what the dog can and cannot eat, they need different food to you. As a parent of younger children, you will be taking on most of the responsibility of the puppy, but you will be able to oversee the bits your children can get involved in and most importantly have fun, puppies are great!

Q. My child has started to regularly use bad language and hand gestures. At first it was kind of funny as it was the first time we had ever heard something so adult out of his mouth. We had the discussion about not using this language or hand gestures and all seemed fine for a while, but it's started again and with more regularity. He is also using it in the right context, and we feel he is seeing this regularly somewhere, possibly in school, but it's not something we do at home. Have you any advice on how we can stop this behaviour as we are concerned that he is using it more often.

A. Kids swear, maybe not in front of you, but they do it. Same with the hand gestures. A lot of parents, the first time they see or hear this behaviour, will laugh as it's not expected and is funny, but this can encourage your child to continue to do it. This can lead to them doing it more regularly and not in the home, which could lead to some embarrassing situations in public.

The solution to the problem is consequences and consistency. The number of parents I work with feel they have very few consequences put in place to deal with their children. There are so many books, tv shows, that give advice, but you need to work out what works best in your home with your children. You, as a parent, probably have several consequences in place in your home already, but just don't see it that way. You already have a way of disciplining your children and you need to continue to use these consequences to correct this new behaviour, but you need to be consistent with them. Perhaps there is a new consequence you could bring in like restricted or no time on a device they like to use such as game console, television or computer. Perhaps they will have to go to bed earlier if they continue to swear. You need to make sure you use these consequences on a tiered basis. If your child swears and it's the first offense, when introducing a consequence there is no point in jumping in with confiscating a device for a week, it won't work. If they swear, give them a warning that if they continue to do so you will introduce a consequence and if they ignore you and keep swearing you can introduce the consequence. The first time should be a reduction in device time or television watching or having to go to bed 15 minutes earlier. If they keep doing it, you keep increasing the amount of time they can't have a device or they will be going to bed earlier and earlier. Eventually they will see that the behaviour is not worth continuing with if they are missing out on game play or tv programmes. Also make sure that anyone involved with your child's routine, e.g. babysitter, grandparents, are aware of what is going on so they can keep the routine going.

Q. What has happened to basic manners in kids? I'm not a parent, but have parents lost the ability to teach their kids manners??

A. It's amazing how the children of every generation are the rudest ever, have no manners or respect for people. Perhaps this generation of children are the rudest, maybe they're not. I think a lot of respect in the past was built out of fear, especially of your elders. When growing up, if I met an adult with my parents and I didn't behave in a fitting manner towards them, I would have got a clip 'round the ear when I got home! I do think that as parents we don't really give our children the understanding of being respectful towards people, young or old.

An important part of bringing up children is teaching them to firstly have respect for themselves, and secondly to have respect for others. If you can manage to do this for your children you've given them a great start in life. You teach them this respect by telling them about it, but more importantly by being respectful to people. Children learn so much more about life through watching their parents and their actions. We don't realise how much our children observe how we behave as adults and then take on board how we deal with situations or people. You need to show your child when someone is being disrespectful, too, so they can see what is wrong with how one person is treating another. Teaching them respect will help in the future when it comes to them using social media and how they portray themselves online and just as importantly how they treat others. It's always good to teach your child the rule of "if you wouldn't say something nasty to someone's face then why is it ok to do it online?" The words are just as hurtful and have a more damaging effect as it could be seen by many other people, too.

Also, as a parent, it is important to teach your children to say "please" and "thank you." A lot of parents don't do this, and those that do will have children who say it to relatives or strangers, but don't say it to each other in the family. It's important that "please" and "thank you" is said to everyone, and, like I mentioned above about teaching your children respect, you have to start as a couple by saying "please" and "thank you" to each other and your children will soon pick up the habit. At home is where all these important simple lessons are learnt but are the backbone to building respectful, caring and considerate humans. You can then go on to teaching them about holding doors open for people or standing back to let someone get by. People are surprised to see children who have manners as it does seem to be less common, but that doesn't have to be the case in your family. Just worry about your own children, how you want them to develop as adults and teach them about respect and manners towards each other first and then people they meet every day.

Q.

Our mornings are an absolute nightmare. Almost every day the kids and I are leaving stressed and angry due to me having to shout at them to get moving. Please help with some ideas to make it easier!

Managing Behaviour

A. Such a common problem for so many parents in the mornings. Kids sleep in, can't find clothes, lunches need to be made. Stress, stress, and more stress.

The way to try and relieve some of this stress is to make changes to the morning routine that are going to help long term, and this may mean tackling some of the morning woes the night before. Making lunches, having uniforms or clothes set out the night before will already be tackling two of the things that need to be done. It will only take 20 minutes to half an hour the evening before to get this done, it won't be stressful, and you can always get your children to help out by setting them the task of getting their clothes ready the night before.

Also go through everything that your child needs for the next day. Have they music or a project due in? Is there a note that needs to go back to the teacher? Having these items in school bags and sorted out the night before is a huge pressure off in the morning.

Next look at your children and see what their behaviour is like in the morning. Sometimes you may have a child who likes to take their time, won't be rushed, and needs a bit more steering in the right direction. If you do have a child like this, it may be worth looking at what time you get up in the morning yourself. It's amazing how much more smoothly things go if you get up 10 minutes earlier.

You may need to wake up the child who takes their time first and offer to help them get dressed. Make sure your children are dressed for school before they come down to the breakfast table as this puts their heads in a different frame of mind straight away. If they are still in their pjs when they are having their breakfast, it's a lot more difficult to get them motivated to go back upstairs and get dressed.

If this is proving difficult then introduce a star chart or reward chart for every morning they get up, dressed, and down for breakfast within a certain amount of time. It shouldn't take long for this routine to become normal and it may feel as if you shouldn't need to reward them for something they should be doing anyway, but as this is new and you are hoping for long term results it may be worth doing for a few weeks. The rewards don't have to be big, just effective.

When breakfast is done this is the time that your child needs to go up and get their teeth brushed, hair done. If there is an older sibling who can help out with hair, then this might be a good time to get them involved.

It may not sound very simple, but it is. It takes a bit of practice and consistency, and you will find that when it all comes together, you will have the time to calmly sit down and have your breakfast together in the morning. Have little chats over breakfast about the day ahead and maybe any plans for the afternoon and you will be leaving the house a lot more relaxed and happy.

There will, of course, be the days when this doesn't happen, and that's life, but if they are the exception and not the rule, then you can happily deal with these days, too. Give it a go and see what happens.

Q. My child constantly interrupts me when I'm talking to other people and it's driving me mad! I don't want to lose it with her in front of other people and embarrass her or the person I'm speaking to, but I'm struggling to deal with it. Any suggestions?

A. Most parents will have dealt with this situation with their children at some point and it can be extremely frustrating, especially if it is done on a regular basis. You can very simply put boundaries in place here and explain to your child that if you are speaking to someone and they need your attention, they firstly say, "Excuse me mum or dad," and wait for you to reply. Now, this seems really simple and it should be easy to put in place, but we are dealing with children who are probably excited or in a hurry to tell us something and don't see the conversation between two adults taking place, they just see you.

It's important that you reinforce this action, even if it takes a few times to get it right. Of course, if it's an emergency this rule doesn't apply, they can say the "excuse me" bit, but need to let you know straight away that it's an emergency and you will need to explain that to them.

Your children need to respect your time and the boundaries. If they come running up to tell you something and don't say "excuse me" first, don't engage with them at all, even if they are pestering. They will soon remember the conversation about interrupting you and will say excuse me first.

You need to make sure that when your child has said "excuse me" and is waiting to talk to you that you speak to them as soon as you can. It's unfair on them that they have done what you asked them to do and now you are just making them stand there and wait until you are ready. This needs to have respect from both sides for it to work, and for your child to know that what they have to say is important to you.

Q. I have three young children and they completely run all over me. I have no control in my own home, and while I love my children, I hate our life at the moment. Please help.

A. It's important that you can admit you are struggling, and you need some help. If, after this bit of advice, you feel you are still struggling, it may be a good idea to seek professional help, perhaps a visit to your GP first and go from there.

It's about boundaries in the house. I'm sure you are all fed up with me saying boundaries, boundaries, boundaries!! They are really important, and next to boundaries in importance are consequences when the boundaries are pushed and completely trampled on.

I have had people say to me that they have boundaries in place that are not being respected and the consequences are not working so what do we do now? If the consequences are not working, then they need to be changed. Something will stick. You may as well have no boundaries in place than ones that don't work. It might be less screen time, having to go to bed earlier, no playing outside with friends that will be the key consequence. They also need to be realistic. Banning a child from no tv for a week or use of a game console will not work. A reduction in time on a device that is increased over the time if the boundaries are not respected will work a lot better, and if they are stuck to, the child will soon learn that the battle isn't worth the loss of the device or tv.

The harder part will come in being consistent with the consequences, especially if you have a child that can be challenging. You need to make sure that the consequence is continued every day that you have put it in place, including the weekends. You will be tired doing it. You are tired already, but the long-term result will be worth it.

You can make a consequence jar for each of your children. You write down consequences for each child and put them in their own labelled jar. You also have a blank consequence, which are the "mercy" consequences. So, this gives you a bit of a break from having to think up the consequence, and if your child misbehaves, they need to go to their jar and pick out a consequence. You can then decide on the length of the consequence depending on the severity of the behaviour. Your child may pick out a "mercy" consequence, but as there will only be one of these, it is unlikely to happen straight off.

You want your children to start to recognise the behaviour that is likely to get a consequence and for them to then make the decision in their head as to whether or not it is worth doing.

Start small and not too heavy as it won't work, and you may end up more stressed and tired than before. Small consequences at first but building if they are not agreeing to stick with it. Start looking at each of your children and write down the behaviour that each child is doing that is causing you to feel overwhelmed and that needs to change. When you have pinpointed the behaviours, you can start to work down through them, but don't try and do all at one time. It's important to work on one at a time for each child and get this turned around before starting on the next one.

If you are consistent, the consequences are effective, and you are willing to put in the time, your children's behaviours will change. Children are usually easier than adults to get them on board with something different.

If you feel your child is too young or perhaps isn't understanding the consequences, then perhaps they need positive reinforcement like a star chart or a reward chart where they can see the results of their positive behaviour.

You need your partner on board, too. There is no point in doing all this hard work and then when your back is turned, your partner has let them watch tv or go out to play. This involves everyone, even grandparents. They might think you are nuts and a bit harsh, but this is about you and how to help you deal with having 3 children to look after and bring up. Sit down and discuss with your partner what happened during the day, what the consequences are, and make sure they are helping you, too.

It's not a quick fix solution, and it will take time and patience to see this through. You will hit the right mark, and everything will run smoothly, but be aware that at some point in the future, as your children reach different stages, they will push against the boundaries again and new consequences will need to be put in place. It may sound very dramatic, it's not. It's just about putting certain things in place that help the family on a day-to-day basis, teaches about respect for everyone, and your children will learn life lessons from the experience.

Boundaries are needed for children ultimately to keep them safe and learn for future life experiences.

Q. My son and daughter have started lying about little things. Not major issues, but just things like brushing their teeth or doing their chores around the house. It doesn't happen all the time and they're pretty good kids, it just frustrates me so much when I know they're lying. Any suggestions?

A. It's one of those things that every child does, but it doesn't mean it's ok or that it's not annoying and winds you up. Everything you do as a parent is trying to bring your children up as good, honest people and here they are lying to you! It's a real issue and something that needs to be nipped in the bud before it becomes a bigger problem. Things like brushing teeth or doing chores may not seem like a big deal to some, but if they are neglecting to do these things now, it can lead to bigger problems in the future. Their dental hygiene is important and it's something that they need to be taking responsibility for as they get older. Doing their bit around the house is important, too, as it's teaching them valuable life lessons for when they have their own homes.

You don't want to get to the point where you have ignored this behaviour, but it is getting to you, and then you explode, and the children have no idea what the problem is. You become so frustrated by what is going on that you may end up imposing a consequence that is bigger than needed and doesn't fit the crime!

If we look at the cycle of conflict, there is the pre-conflict where there is something that brings on the conflict like the continuing lying. Then we have the triggering event, and then we have the argument, and then we have the resolution. We, as adults, can stop this cycle going full circle by implementing the boundary by telling them they must brush their teeth, watching over them initially every time they need to do it so that they are doing it and doing it correctly. You are letting them know that you are not going to let them get away with firstly not brushing their teeth, and secondly lying about it when asked. Sometimes, we get to the point as parents when we feel that we shouldn't really have to be standing over our children and making sure they do certain things, and that's true. You shouldn't, but if they are not doing it, you need to treat them like a younger child. They will get fed up of you standing over them watching every time they brush their teeth or whatever it is they lied about doing or not doing. They will get to the point when they will tell you they've learned their lesson and promise to do as they are asked, but they are children, and more than likely this behaviour will happen again. But for now, you need to trust them, give them a bit of leeway, and enjoy that everything is running a bit more smoothly then normal! Children need to mess up, make mistakes, and you need to create the boundaries and safe environment for them to do this as they will learn from these mistakes and hopefully carry the experience with them. It's a pain, it's repetitive, but that's your job as a parent. Put the realistic consequence in place, be consistent with it, and more than likely in a week or two this issue will be sorted, for now!

Q. My nephew never says "please" or "thank you," and it drives me nuts. Neither my sister nor her partner corrects him. I think basic manners are essential. Is it my place to do anything?

A. Basic manners are something that are so simple for a child to learn and for parents or other family members to teach. It's amazing how quickly a child will learn these lessons, especially if it results in something good coming of it like receiving a treat or getting to play a favourite game.

In the youth project I work in, I get the teenagers to use their "please" and "thank you's" and make it very clear to them that they won't get to do an excursion or get certain food if they don't use their manners. It's about respect, too. If I say "please" and "thank you" to you, it would be right that you say it back to me.

Not all parents teach their children manners, and a lot of the time it is because they don't do it themselves, towards each other or towards other people. It's not up to the children to figure out how to show respect, they need to be shown how to do it. Perhaps their parents don't know how to do it, perhaps they are afraid of their child's reaction or behaviour if asked.

So, what you can do is make sure that when they are in your company, whether it's your house or their house, anywhere, he needs to learn to say "please" and "thank you." He needs to learn that he won't get something if he doesn't use these words. You will find that if you are consistent with him, he will start to use them regularly, and possible with his parents, too, who may well keep it up.

As an adult, you can be a positive influence on him, and he will have respect for you and vice versa. These lessons will help him through life, especially as he enters higher levels of school and eventually the workplace.

Just make sure that you put the consequence in place if he doesn't say "please" or "thank you."

Q. I have a wonderful, little 8-year-old boy who is great fun and generally really well-behaved. I've started to notice a few euro going missing here and there, and finding unexplainable sweet wrappers in the bedroom, as well as small toys in the house that we definitely haven't bought him. It looks like he's stealing a bit of money. How do I deal with this in the right way?

A. This is something that most parents will deal with during their children growing up, and it's usually very minor. It may be the odd couple of euro here or there, or some loose change you have left lying about, and it's not something to overreact about. It's another part of life that your child will be learning about. They may not know that it's not right to take money that was not given to them, or to ask before they take money. Don't overreact, this does not mean or indicate that your child is going into a life of crime and thievery.

You need to have a discussion with your son and explain to him that you've noticed that there has been some money missing and that you've noticed he has some new toys that you didn't buy for him, sweets he's been eating. He may straight away deny that they are his, that a friend gave them to him, which would be the natural thing to do, but you know your son, and you will be able to read his reaction as being truthful or not. It's an opportunity to have a discussion with him about stealing and why it's not right to do it no matter how big or small the item may be. If it is something that continues to happen, you may need to bring in consequences as you have discussed with him that it is not right, and he has decided to continue to take money.

Don't set a trap or test your son to see if your child has decided not to steal anymore by leaving money lying around, this isn't fair on your child. You are trying to build a trusting relationship with your son, and you have to believe that he has taken on board what you have said to him, and he will do the right thing. If money does go missing, have the conversation again with your son. He is learning and will repeat certain behaviour a number of times before he gets that it's wrong. Many adults repeat the same silly behaviour all the time and don't learn from their mistakes. Consequences will be needed but need to match the behaviour. Always start with small consequences at first, like an earlier bedtime or reduced time on a device, this usually is enough for things to change. If this doesn't work, you will need to increase the time or even confiscate a certain game, device. The consequences need to fit the behaviour. Just monitor the behaviour, keep the consequences relative, and build the trust with your child.

Q. We were having a fun chat with our children, and who the fav parent was, and my youngest daughter said "60% daddy and 40% mammy, 'cause daddy is more fun." It was a light-hearted conversation, but it got me thinking about how I'm usually the bad cop in the house and I know it's mainly because I'm around the kids more than my husband. How can my husband take more of a roll in the discipline in the house?

A. This is probably the same in many households around the world. In most houses, it is the mother who has the most contact with the children on a day-to-day basis, and therefore has to deal with more of the disciplinary action and be the harder parent, as it were. The positive of being around your children is that you are probably 90% good cop when you are with them, having fun and letting them do things that perhaps their dad wouldn't let them do. You just may not notice this as sometimes it can feel as if you are continuously giving out to someone. I get the impression that this isn't an issue that is keeping you up at night, but when you are the parent that is having to deal with most of the discipline in the house, it can become frustrating, and if you are tired and run down, it could become an issue.

Have a chat with your husband about how you are feeling. You are not trying to get a 50/50 balance in the house as you know this isn't possible but try and get him on board with a bit more of the discipline when he is around. See if he could take over in the evenings or the weekend, this is the time when you could do with a break. Sit down and come up with a plan—dad will still be fun dad, but they will see that he is also responsible for discipline in the house and they will appreciate it in the long run.

Your children need to know what is ok and not ok with their dad, too, on the small and the big issues. It doesn't have to be over the top or heavy handed, but it will be a break for you from having to give out and punish a child. You may need to let your husband know the triggers in the evenings and at the weekend that are an issue for you so he is aware of them and can step in. This may take a couple of weeks to get right as he may not see the behaviour as a problem, and if he hasn't been disciplining the child much up to this point, he might miss some things. He needs to be aware that you have been dealing with the same issues all week with the children, so although he may only be experiencing it for the first time, you may have dealt with it a number of times during the week and that can be very frustrating and lead to arguments.

I'm sure your husband will be more than happy to help, take the load off you a bit, and give you a break before Monday comes around again.

Q. My 14-year-old literally walks around all day and scowls at everyone in the house. He used to be such a happy child but seems to be really angry towards us and his sister. Is this normal and what can we do to make him less angry?

A. 14 years-of-age is the toughest age for children. You are physically changing and going through all sorts of hormonal changes, but your brain development isn't at the same age and it can be difficult to emotionally deal with all that is going on in your body. This is the normal development at this age. When you are 14, you may feel you are physically bigger, maybe bigger than your parents, and this could give you a feeling of control or superiority over them. You no longer fit into the "child' bracket," but you are not yet an adult. Your child will be forming their own opinions on what they want for their lives and may battle more with you to get what they want.

Hormonal changes make it so difficult for teenagers to express how they are feeling, one minute it's all good, the next it could be the end of the world. It's extremely frustrating for them as well as for you. There is a lot of getting to know this new person, getting used to the physical and mental changes.

There is also the issue with social media, which creates another layer of pressure on teenagers in the world they live in now. You all want to belong in a group, but you are supposed to have an individuality too. It's a tough time for parents too. If your child walked around happy for most of their life, and all of a sudden, their personality has done a 180 turn, you are unsure what is going on.

There needs to be a level of respect on both sides. Your son cannot go around being off with everyone because that's how he is feeling. Also, you need to respect the changes happening and be mindful of this. You will need to put up with a certain amount of moody behaviour, and perhaps little interaction with your child at this age, but if he is being rude, disrespectful, and upsetting members of the family, that's not ok and you will need to address this.

This is when the consequences need to come in. You need to look at what would be effective consequences for your son. They need to make him stop and look at his behaviour and then control it so that he won't be without his phone, computer. The mobile phone is usually the most effective consequence for parents to put in place, but you may need to have others in place too. Does he play PlayStation, hang out late with his friends? These are all things that can be restricted until your son learns to look at himself and his behaviour and correct it so it's not having such an impact on your family.

You could get your son involved in some voluntary work or send them off to grandparents to help out around the house. Their behaviour won't be tolerated, they will learn some new skills, and they won't be hanging around the house. He may not want to do it, but he is 14 years-of-age and really has no choice.

There needs to be a bit of a balance. Your son cannot be disrespectful, but he needs some room too, so he can process all the madness in his head.

SAFETY
(ONLINE & OFFLINE)

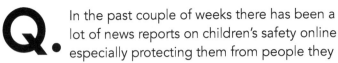

Q. In the past couple of weeks there has been a lot of news reports on children's safety online especially protecting them from people they can't see and may not be who they say they are. What can we do to safeguard our children online especially when they are not in our company?

A. This is a drum I've been beating for quite a while about having a discussion with your children about online safety. It's as important as the conversations you will have with your children about drugs, alcohol and sex. It's not just about predators, it's also about how our children behave online. Depending on the age of your child it may be worth looking at putting a screening device on your child's phone or tablet. This is something that parents can have an issue over in terms of their child's privacy and not snooping on them. It's peace of mind for many parents that they can check their child's interactions when they are online and check who they are making contact with. We need to take responsibility for our children, we need to keep them safe. We wouldn't dream of sending them outside with complete strangers, it's no different online. Don't worry about what other children are doing online or what other parents allow their children to do, you need to look after your own children.

You need to have the conversation with your children about the content they put online especially photos or private information about themselves. Children can be very innocent when it comes to the sharing of information/photos online and do not realise how quickly this can then be shared with people they do not know. Ask them is what they are putting online something they would want their grandparent to see or know about or even just their parents. They need to be aware that as soon as they put something online it's there forever regardless of the type of privacy you may have set on their social media. In a lot of social media apps in their terms and conditions they own the rights to any photos you post online. Recent studies have found that a large percentage of photographs found on child pornography sites have originally been taken from people's social media pages. It's quite shocking. This is not said to scare or stop people from using the internet, it is an amazing well of information for so many of us, but it needs to be monitored. You need to have the conversation that you will be monitoring their use of the internet. This is not to spy on them, it's to keep them safe. You need to keep a calmness if they accidentally access a site they shouldn't be in, this happens and it's very easy for inappropriate images/information to be included in an innocent web search by a child. You need to let them know that they can talk to you if they are worried about something they have seen online or if someone is trying to contact them online and the conversation is not appropriate, or it is worrying them. This also applies to how people they know are treating them online too (e.g. classmates, friends in their neighbourhood).

It's important to have the discussion about how they conduct themselves online, the language they use, and whether or not they would say the same things to someone's face. It's very easy to put down in a text message or tweet how you really feel about someone, but would you say that to them? Are they aware of the impact their words could have on the person receiving them?

You need to make sure they are not having too much screen time, especially at home. We can't worry about the rest of the world, what other families are doing. We need to just concentrate on our own family.

Q. My 6-year-old plays outside with his friends all the time. We live in an estate with lots of other kids and it's fantastic as my kids have loads of friends. Our worry is that our son told us that a man approached them while walking his dog and offered them some sweets. It has made us and our neighbours very nervous. How do I talk to my son about stranger danger without scaring the daylights out of him?

A. Your last line is very significant. We can tell our children to never speak to strangers but one day we could meet an old acquaintance that our child doesn't know, and they refuse to answer their questions as to them this person is a stranger!

Safety

It's about teaching them about awareness and also the age of the child will dictate the language you use. If your child is younger than 6, they shouldn't be somewhere that a responsible adult is not aware of what they are doing or watching them.

At age 6, there are boundaries in terms of where they can go, perhaps not out of sight of the house or behind others houses. It may just be that this man was saying 'hello' and being kind, but it's better to err on the side of caution.

You need to make it clear to your child that they are never to go off with someone who asks them to, regardless of the reason why. They may use reasons such as to help them out or that they have puppies in their car or house, and would your child like to see them. This includes people that they know too, family or friends. Your child needs to tell the adult that no they can't go; they need to chat to their mum or dad first. The majority of cases of kidnap or abuse towards children is done by someone that is known to the child. Even if the adult has said to the child that they spoke to their parents, the child needs to tell them that they have to check with them also.

Your child needs to know that even if the person seems nice, they should never go off with anyone and always need to come to you to check. You as a parent need to be regularly checking where your child is too, look out for them, check they are in sight.

The chances of anything happening are very slim but you need to make your child aware and give them the tools to get out of a situation. We always tell our girls never to go off with anyone—friend, family or stranger—and if they are not comfortable with the situation they are to scream and run away as fast as possible.

Q. My daughter's friend is always over at our house. She's a great kid and lovely to have around. I'm a bit concerned that she's always looking for food. She's quite a slight child and seems a bit small for her age, but I'm worried maybe she isn't getting enough food at home. I'm not sure how to talk to her mum about it or even if I should. Any advice?

A. It's great having your child's friends around the house as it means you get to know them better and find out a lot about your own child too, probably more than they tell you. As time goes on as with any relationship, you will start to notice more about this child, and perhaps your instincts have kicked in and you are now concerned about her as her behaviour of asking for food increases or becomes a regular occurrence.

Some children are just monsters when it comes to food, have fast metabolisms and need to graze all day. On the flip side, it could be the opposite, they could be slight and small because they are not receiving the nutritional needs to meet their growth. It's ok to have this concern and it is going to be a really difficult discussion with their parents if you feel it is needed. It depends a lot on the relationship you have with this mum. Is it friendly, and do you speak regularly, or do you only have contact when dropping off or picking up children?

Perhaps make a light-hearted joke about the amount of food the kids eat in your house to the mum and ask casually is she the same in theirs? You might get a 'yeah exactly the same' or 'no she doesn't eat that much at all.' This will help you get a bit more of an idea but not a definitive answer.

If after you are still concerned about the child's nutrition, it may be worth getting some advice from social services as to what to do. This may sound drastic, but if you are concerned, then something needs to be done. You don't need to give over any names or information, but it may help to ask those difficult questions. Your school may already have concerns about this.

You could always ask your daughter about the friend's lunches or when they are in their house what do they eat but be subtle and do it in a casual manner.

Q. My 8-year-old daughter has a good friend in our neighborhood. She plays with her friend and her brother often, both at our house and at theirs. We aren't super close with her parents but are acquaintances.

A couple weeks ago, the kids were playing at our house,

it was getting late and I sent them home. Twenty minutes later, there was a knock at the door, it was the mom with the kids, they were all in tears and something was very clearly wrong.

When I asked questions, the mom said she and her husband had been having difficulty getting along and her husband has been drinking a lot, and they had just gotten into a huge fight. During the fight, her husband snapped her phone in half and threw it at her, missing her and it went through a window. The kids were present when this happened. They left and came to our house immediately after.

The mom did not want to involve the police but seemed clearly afraid of her husband. She eventually went home, and the kids ended up staying at our house for the evening. When I brought them home, both parents were there and the vibe in the house made me super uncomfortable.

Once the dust settled on the situation, it was a good opportunity to talk with my girls about being in respectful relationships, that it's not okay for anyone to hurt or intimidate you, or for you to feel afraid of your partner, or vice versa. My kids have never been exposed to anything like this and I would love to get your thoughts on how to talk with kids and better reinforce the topic.

Additionally, given the current situation, I'm finding myself concerned about having my daughter play at their house. if there was another angry/violent outbreak, I wouldn't feel good about my daughter being present or caught in the middle. We're allowing our daughter to play with her friend but only at our house. I don't think I'm overreacting but would love to get your thoughts. Also, the new rules have brought up questions from our daughter as to why she can't play at her friend's house and I'm not sure how much detail to go into with her. Any advice you have is very welcome!

A. Very tough situation for all involved and there are so many elements that are out of your control. Let's look at your relationship with this couple first. You say you are not very close, just acquaintances and only as a result of your children being friends. It's difficult when a situation like this comes up and you don't know how to react. You are not involved in this family's life, so you are unsure as to how long these problems have been going on and sometimes you don't know whether or not to give advice or to just be an ear to listen. The most important thing is that we all have a duty of care to the children and we need to make sure that we feel ok and confident that the children are safe. Of course, you will have concerns for the mum too, but she is an adult and more able to protect herself than the children can, it is more in her control.

You could ask her if she comes to you again if she needs some advice or would like your help. Perhaps she needs to take a break from her husband for a few days, space apart to sort out what is going on and allow some calmness to the situation. Maybe her partner could go visit family for a few days and try and make sense of what is happening.

People will find it easy to pass remarks on other people's relationships and family life, and that's easy to do when you are looking in from the outside, but it's not the reality of anyone's life. It's very different when you are in a relationship that is going through a difficult time for whatever reason. You have been with this person for a long time and shared so many experiences with each other. You want it to work, you want a happy family, and sometimes you will put yourself through tough situations to try and keep things going. It is a time when this family won't need other people's opinions, just support.

If she is feeling uncomfortable or under threat, she will need to deal with this and get herself and her children to a safe place to stay or have her partner removed from the house, but this is something she will need to instigate herself.

Back to the children. You need to know if they are safe in the house. You may feel it's not something you should be getting involved in, but if anything happened to those children and you didn't act on your initial concerns over their safety, you wouldn't forgive yourself. If this becomes a reoccurring situation or you feel that the children are in danger, you will need to report this to the authorities. It is a big step and there is no going back on the decision, but you will need to get in touch with your local police or social services and explain the situation to them. People may find out that you discussed this with the authorities. The family may find out and not be too pleased, but the only thing that matters is the children's safety.

You have done really well so far in supporting the family, taking the children out of the situation for the night and giving them some peace. Next you need to have the discussions with your children about what is going on. This can start around relationships and what a healthy, happy relationship means to you. What is acceptable and not acceptable in a relationship. Your children are young and therefore nothing too serious needs to be discussed. Use simple terms and language and don't go into anything that may frighten them or give them concerns about their own family set up. They won't be able to put any of this into context and it may only confuse and upset them.

The biggest conversations you will need to have now is the one with your daughter as to why she can't go to her friend's house to play. You are not overreacting by not letting her go to the house, especially as the mother has told you there are issues in the family at present and no parent would put their child in danger. This will pass and things will change, and your daughter will go over to her friend's house again, but you will need to see if the dad is there and will it be ok. You will need to keep an eye on the situation there for the time being.

You will have to have the discussion with your child about what happened and how important their safety is to you. They will need to know that arrangements will be a bit different for a little while, but it's to keep her safe and these are the rules for a bit. Don't go too deep with her about it, it's a need-to-know situation and she will just have to follow the rules. You are not stopping her from playing with her friend, it just needs to be done differently for a while.

Q.

My 13-year-old daughter came to us and showed us a picture she'd been sent on her phone of a boy in her class, exposed from the waist down. She was really upset by this and doesn't want us to say anything to anyone. What should we do?

A.

That's something that is becoming more and more common where teenagers are being sent and are sending inappropriate images from/to others. Our mobile phones are not just phones like the good old days, they are mobile computers. Us adults use our phones so many times a day and it's become normal, but for our children, we need to take control of the device and how they use it. If they are in their young teen years you wouldn't allow your child to disappear for hours on end without knowing what or who they are with and it's the same with their phones. They should not have hours of unsupervised use of their mobile phones/computers.

The image your daughter received on her phone was distressing for her, she did not ask for it, and it should never have been sent to her. There is a big discussion to have with our children in relation to consent online. What is ok and not ok to do online, what are the things you would never do in real life and should therefore not do online. The boy who sent the image would never hand over a printed copy of it to your daughter in person.

We need to have the conversation with our children about what they may be exposed to when they get a mobile phone/tablet, and to let you know when it happens so it can be dealt with correctly.

There are laws in relation to the distribution of pornographic images, which if needed, can involve the police/garda. It may seem extreme considering this is involving children, but your daughter has rights and the image sent could be seen as illegal content and prosecution can occur.

You may need to involve the school that the children go to, or if you know the parents of the boy, you need to have a conversation with them. This type of behaviour needs to be corrected and stopped from happening again. The school may not want to get involved, but they may appreciate knowing about the behaviour as they will have experienced this behaviour amongst their students.

The conversation about online consent and behaviour is as important to have with your child as talking to them about drugs and sex. You will need to gauge the stage they are at and make the conversation appropriate to them, otherwise they will become overwhelmed and will have information that may upset or confuse them. Our children are growing up in an environment of uncertainty. They may see pornographic images/videos and feel this is the way to have a normal sexual relationship and that they need to live up to this. They may be very embarrassed about the conversation, but they will be glad of it in the long run. We can only look after our own children and their welfare, not anyone else's. Therefore, it is important that we control their online behaviour and try to educate them on how to navigate the internet safely and responsibly.

Q. My son is getting his first mobile phone for Christmas and both me and my husband are nervous about him getting it. What advice can you give us around how to manage this as best we can?

A. First things first, you have a bit of time to do your homework in terms of safeguarding your child while they are using their phone. You can start to have conversations with your child about the boundaries that will be put in place in regard to use of the phone. Talk through the rules, these will be there to keep your child safe and not to put a damper on them getting a phone. Talk about the apps they may like to have on their phone. I'm not sure how old your child is, but a number of apps have age restrictions and if you are not happy with your child getting a particular app then you can let them know that you won't be downloading it on their phone and that they won't be able to do it themselves.

We can give in to our kids so easily and we don't want them to feel that they are being left out, but if you give your child unlimited access to social media with no restrictions, they are going to see content that is not suitable, that their brains will not be able to process. So if you are going to let your child use social media, what are they allowed to access, is it suitable and what are the boundaries you are going to put in place to keep their social media usage safe?

There are a number of apps that you can download to monitor your child's use of social media. It can look for words, images that your child may have received in texts and messages and see if they are inappropriate and need to be highlighted. This not only lets you keep them safe from others, but it's a great way to see how your child is conducting themselves on social media too. Your child will need to be aware that once something is sent out there, it's out there, and even if you delete the message from your phone, it's still available on the internet.

If you are allowing your child access to the internet you may want to restrict what they can look at. We all want our children to be aware of the world around us, but they can also be a couple of clicks away from viewing material such as porn or murder that's not appropriate and may cause anxiety in your child. It is very simple to restrict the content your child is allowed to search online, and they may need to ask your permission to allow them to view a certain site. It may seem crazy to have to monitor their searches, but the internet is a very interesting place, it is both good and bad, and as a parent you want your child to get all the positives out of it until they are old enough and mature enough to know what the downside of the internet is.

If you put the work in now, have the conversations with your child about the phone and the boundaries, you are less likely to have arguments in the future. Having a phone is a big step on the ladder of growing up and you need to trust that your child will be responsible. Have the conversation about how they conduct themselves online, in texts and messages, and also to be careful about the information they give out to others—especially personal information. They may think they are just having a one-on-one conversation with a friend when in actual fact the whole world can have access to their messages. Any information they put online is there forever, so they need to think twice before they post something. Also, if they can see online bullying going on in a chat they are in, make sure they don't get involved. Let them know that you are there for them to discuss what they may have read and how they feel about it. If it's something serious, a parent may need to get involved.

Keep chatting to your child about the phone, what they are doing, and keep reminding them about the boundaries. Try not to let them on it all the time, have phone breaks, and not to have the phone in the bedroom at night even if they are only using it as an alarm!!

SEPARATION
& DIVORCE

Q.

I've been separated from my husband for a while now and have met someone new and things are going well. I'm not sure what is the best time and how to introduce him to my twin boys. Have you any advice?

A.

This is something that a lot of parents struggle with. When to introduce my children to a new partner and what I need to look out for to make sure my children are ok with this new person in their lives. One of the big things in a separation is to be mindful of the children's feelings towards both of you. They love both of you equally and it's not their fault that you separated. Those issues are between you and your ex-partner. It's important that they get to see both parents as just that, both their parents and not feel that one or the other is being replaced by a new partner.

Don't rush into it especially if it's only a new relationship. You need to make sure that this person is going to be a permanent fixture in all your lives. It's not ideal to introduce a new partner too soon and then the relationship doesn't work out and then there might be a new person who you want to introduce. Contact your ex-partner and let them know that you are in a new relationship so that the children can talk about it with them and not feel it is a secret. It's amazing how many times children of separated parents feel the need to protect one or the other parent and keep things to themselves in order not to hurt that parent or get in trouble. This can lead to the children becoming anxious and worried. Even if you don't have a good relationship with your ex just drop a quick text explaining that you are in a new relationship and it's time to let the children know.

Next you can sit down with your children and explain to them that you are in a new relationship with someone that you really care for and they care for you too. Explain that you would like to introduce them to this person but there is no pressure, it would be a very causal meeting, not in the house, as this can make kids feel uneasy and just see how you get on. You can't rush this. The first meeting shouldn't be in the house or letting the kids know that this person is going to move in with them straight away, it's too soon and too much for kids to process. Let them know that you are aware that this may seem strange to them and that's ok, and also that their other parent knows this is happening, so they won't feel that it's a secret from the other parent. They need to know that they are the most important part of all of this, they need to feel secure. Take it slowly, I'm sure this will be just as nerve wracking for you too.

New relationships can be very exciting at first, and if this is someone you plan on spending a lot of time with, the relationship will change and develop. It may seem unfair that you can't just enjoy this new relationship, but you have children and they matter most, so it's good to take it slowly as everyone gets used to this new situation. Allow your children to ask any questions they feel they need answered, even the difficult ones! They may want to know if this is their new mum or dad. It's a tough question but if this person becomes a permanent member of your family there will be decisions over discipline, boundaries. I'm not trying to scare anyone, but this is a massive new development and needs a lot of thinking and time to get it right. If you rush into this relationship and introduce someone too soon who then feels they can discipline your children or treat your children in a manner that is not right, you can have all sorts of problems with your children and also your ex-partner who may hear stories about the treatment to their children and not be happy about it.

If you are the new person in the relationship, you need to have patience and take your time too. You need to be mindful of the children and the time it might take for everyone to be ok with the new relationship. If this person means that much to you and you feel this is a relationship you want to last, then you will need to respect them and the children and the fact that this will be very new for everyone.

Q. My ex-wife and I had a difficult break up and she has basically stopped me from seeing my children. The way I feel about it is that our issues are between us and not to do with our kids, but she seems to be using the kids to get at me. I'm really missing my kids and all I want is to see them. We are in court, but it's such a slow process. I'm at a loss as to what to do.

A. This is such a difficult situation to be in. This is becoming more of a real-life problem, especially for a number of dads I work with. I'm not saying it's only dads who experience this in a separation, but the majority of clients I have dealing with this issue are dads. They are not seeing their children for months and the children are being used to punish the parent who doesn't have custody of them. You are working through the court process and it is a very slow process. The judge may be looking for assessments to be done or investigations into your background, this can push back any decisions on custody or visiting rights which increases the amount of time that you have not seen your children.

Try as hard as you can to maintain some contact with your children: write a letter, or if possible, a phone call. It will mean a lot to them and they will know that you are still there for them. Make sure your solicitor or barrister is keeping on top of the process so as not to incur more delays. Keep a journal, note how your day went so your kids can read over the time you were apart and see if they can do the same for you. Write about your interests, what you've been doing, and that you are thinking of them all the time and can't wait to see them again. It's very difficult, they will be missing you too, and you have no control over how you are being portrayed by others. You may be the parent who has been hurt because your partner had an affair or did something that has led to this point, but it has nothing to do with the children. It's not the children's fault.

Try and use a child-centred approach, focus on what is important for the child, and then you can start to see it from the child's perspective. Don't deprive the child of seeing someone they love and is important in their lives because you are angry with them and want to hurt them. It's really important to take the time and deal with your feelings. It's perfectly ok to feel hurt and to know you have issues with this person as you have split up and they hurt you, but don't let these feelings drive what is your children's relationship with their other parent.

Kids pick up on how you interact with the other parent although you may feel you are not acting that way. Your body language, tone of voice, or even lack of communication tells your children a lot about how you are feeling towards the other person. When you are dealing with this issue, play out in your head how you are going to communicate with your ex-partner. It won't be easy, but for the sake of your children you will need to try and practice this. You may even need to go and see someone to help you through these communications with your ex-partner.

Your kids need to see both parents being respectful to each other, it's how they learn about respect towards people and getting respect from people too. If they are not experiencing this in their own lives, they may feel they don't need to respect people.

It's a difficult situation to be in, frustrating for all involved, but taking simple steps can help all the relationships involved and will hopefully result in amicable meetings with your ex- partner and more time with your children.

Q. I'm recently separated from my husband. Our children live with me and see their dad at the weekends. Things between us aren't great. I'm going on holidays with my sister in the summer as I need a break and my ex is taking the kids for a week. I don't want there to be too much upheaval for them but how do I get ex to keep the normal routine going for the kids for the week.

A. We regularly discuss what it's like to be a separated parent as it's a much more common situation in many families. For a lot of children, they are now used to living in different houses at different times with either parent and a lot of the time the parents have a good relationship especially for the benefit of the children.

We cannot control what the other parent does. If you have a difficult relationship with your ex, what you may find is that you want your children to have the normal routine, and you mention this to your ex and they most probably will scrunch it up and put it in the bin as soon as your back is turned. They will see this as an opportunity not to obey you and to let you know that they will parent the children any way they want as they are staying with them and not you. This happens, I've had experience with it with separated couples.

There is so much pain, hurt, anger between some couples after they separate, and they sometimes forget to see the bigger picture which is the upbringing of their children that they had together.

Some ex-partners will take their frustration out on their ex by using the children and putting them in uncomfortable and upsetting situations just to make a point. They haven't done anything to cause the break-up, they are not to blame so don't make them feel like it's their fault. They are not a pawn to be used in a game of getting back at an ex-partner who has hurt us.

It is, of course, a good idea that your children have the same routine in your house as they do in their dad's house. It creates stability for them and lets them see that although you are not together as a couple, you are still jointly parenting the children. You can sit down with your ex and go through the routine with him and let him know about it. You could approach him by saying it would be great for the kids if you could keep the routine for as much as possible. I'm sure you have things planned for them and that's great, but the bedtimes are really important as are the mealtimes. You can do this and trust that your partner will do it, but if it's not, don't use it as a stick to beat your ex with. Suggest it but know that they may have different plans for the children while they are with them. As we all know with children, if they don't have a routine in place, it can all go very wrong very quickly and your ex may be more than happy to have the routine to follow instead of dealing with over-tired, hungry, and upset children.

What can happen in a lot of separated couples is the parent who has the children most of the time is the disciplinarian and the other parent is the "fun" parent, and with situations like this, it will be good for the "fun" parent to have to discipline the children too. There needs to be a balance in place. When your children are young, they need a parent not a best friend. That relationship comes when your children are older, and you no longer need to parent them as they are adults. It will be good for your ex to have to take on some of the discipline.

Your children will be fine, they will be looked after, and have a great time as will you. They will be delighted to see you when you get back, and you will have a much needed and deserved break from each other!

Q. Myself and my ex-husband just can't seem to get along. I'm really hurt as he had an affair and he tries to make out that it was the way I treated him that pushed him away. I'm really worried that this is impacting on our 8-year-old daughter who has become really quiet and withdrawn. I try to talk to my ex about it, but he just dismisses it as normal kid stuff. Is there anything I can do to support her and get her to come back out of her shell?

A. This is a very worrying situation for any parent, separated or together. Sometimes what we find is if there has been a separation when an affair has been the reason for the split there can be anger towards the person who has hurt you and it overrides the love for the children. It's not done on purpose, it's just one of those situations where this kind of behaviour manifests itself.

Firstly, the difficulty you have with your ex-husband is something you need to look to resolve within yourself. The affair cannot be undone, the way you have been treated cannot be reversed, unfortunately, and obviously the way your ex feels about your relationship and the break-up cannot be changed either. But what is most important is that you as parents and adults can get some stability in your relationship to make your children feel safe. We need to remember that when parents separate, children can feel so many different emotions such as guilt, sadness, hurt, and even relief—especially if the relationship has been full of arguments and shouting. It's really important to look at how you are going to give your children a solid foundation as you both move on in separate directions even though you yourself are hurting too. If you are struggling emotionally with the breakup of your relationship, go and get some professional help, it is worth it. Some people are put off by the financial strain of attending a professional counsellor, but the money you pay is well worth it for your mental health and how that will in turn help you to deal with other situations in a healthier, balanced, and calm way.

In regard to your daughter, if you are very concerned about her change in behaviour, you could seek the help of a professional child counsellor. Firstly, you yourself can look at what you can do to help your child feel safe and create a stable atmosphere for them. You can't do anything about your partner, how he parents, what he does when they have time together, and that can be really frustrating. You could be in a situation where you have the children with you all week and have to deal with the school runs, homework, activities, dinners, and then they see their dad at the weekend and it's all about the fun. It may seem as if there is an extra demand on you to do all the serious parenting stuff and dad is having all the fun and is more fun to be around. You need to accept that this is the way it is and unless your partner is going to go through mediation with you, or sit down and discuss with you rationally how you are going to raise the children when separated, you need to focus on what you can do in your home to make your children feel safe and happy during this difficult time. Your daughter could be worried about your interactions with her dad, especially if there has been a tendency for arguments. Children can pick up on tension and may not know how to deal with it emotionally or explain to you verbally and they may withdraw. She may be trying to protect herself and is trying to stay out of the way, so she is not adding to the argument. You and your ex need be aware of this and try and conduct your conversations in a calm manner.

You could give your daughter a notebook and let her write down how she is feeling, she can then show this to you or just keep it for herself. Ask her how she is feeling, but don't press her. Bring it up when the focus isn't necessarily on her, so when you are driving her somewhere or you are doing an activity like baking together. She might just say she is fine, she may not write anything, but keep giving her the opportunities to talk but not be under pressure.

Look at spending fun time together, look at her interests and ask can you get involved too. If she is in a funny mood and doesn't want to go outside with her friends or do an activity, make her. Stick her outside to play and within a couple of minutes she will be running around and enjoying herself. She might be annoyed at first, but it will soon be forgotten.

Look at how you do what you do. If you are talking about dad, make sure that you are watching what you are saying and the tone used, especially if there is a chance that she could overhear you.

You could write a commitment letter to your child to let her know

Separation & Divorce

that she had nothing to do with the breakup. Let her know that you, as her parents, have talked about the details of how the breakup will work so that it affects her as little as possible and you have her best interests at heart and want her to feel safe and secure. A letter is something she can hold on to and read, especially if she is feeling a bit down and insecure about what is happening to her family. Maybe your ex could do the same too, or maybe you could do it together if the relationship will allow.

It's a really tough situation you are in especially if the relationship with your ex-partner is not amicable. Your daughter's safety and well-being are the most important things and you need to create an atmosphere that helps her to also deal with this big change in your lives.

TEENS

Q. What should a single mum do who has a teenage son who is now bigger than her and pushing her about thinking he is the boss and dictating the pace at home?

A. Being physically aggressive in any relationship is not ok. No parent should be physically aggressive towards their child, and no child should be physically aggressive towards their parent.

You need to take a look at the actual behaviour and what he is doing. Is he being physically aggressive, verbally aggressive, and if he is not responding to the consequences you have put in place as a result of his behaviour, you need to look at external supports that can help you. This support could come from an uncle, aunt, grandparent that your child looks up to and respects no matter what. You could ask them to have a conversation with your child about their behaviour and how it is not acceptable.

If this doesn't work and your child is becoming increasingly aggressive towards you in a physical manner, you can always contact your local Garda station. If he has no boundaries to stop him from behaving this way, you may need a stronger voice to explain to him clearly the line he has crossed and if he continues to cross this line they can set out clearly the line the Garda will take with him. They may even caution him as a first step.

You may need to look at the consequences in place at home. Sometimes a parent will try and keep the peace in the house to avoid the confrontation, they may give in to them and this then rewards the negative behaviour. Like with small children, any attention, even negative, is better than no attention. Do not reward the negative behaviour. Get supports in place to help you. No parent wants to get the Garda involved, but if they are physically aggressive towards another person in their early teens, it is up to you to rectify this behaviour. If your child leaves home at 18 and you have lived with this behaviour without tackling it, they may go on to be physically aggressive towards a partner or child or get into fights. You need to help your child in their teens to deal with this behaviour and it will be better for you and your child in the long term.

Q. My teenage daughter's behaviour is getting more and more worrying. She is not listening to me and I'm worried that she is taking drugs. She stays out late and I'm really struggling with boundaries. Her father and I have been separated a long time, but we have a really good relationship and work well together. He's trying to help as much as he can, but what can we do to get our daughter on track?

A. This is a positive relationship although they are separated. They are working together and are on the same page when it comes to bringing up their daughter. It brings up an interesting point that we can work as hard as we can as parents, but sometimes it doesn't work out well, or it goes off the rails a bit. It is very difficult sometimes to be a parent of a teenage child. They are at a point when they want to pull away from us and exercise their independence, but unfortunately, they are still very young and not mature enough or have enough life skills to deal with certain situations they may find themselves in.

You are separated but have a clear idea of how you want to bring up your daughter. This is a time when you really need to come together, all under the same roof, for a discussion with your daughter and set out the boundaries. Let her know what is and is not acceptable behaviour, these are the consequences for their behaviour. If they have a curfew and they are continuing to stay out beyond it, you reduce the time they are allowed to stay out. So, if the curfew is 9.30pm and they are half-an-hour late back, reduce it to 9pm. Or if it's an hour late back, reduce it by an hour and keep going until they get the message that their bad behaviour will not be rewarded. It doesn't have to be big to have an impact, but it has to be consistent. You can confiscate devices (i.e. phone, laptop) if you feel this will have the desired impact on their behaviour.

The issue with the drugs is becoming more common amongst parents and their teenage children. Teenagers will experiment with alcohol, cigarettes, drugs. If it is a worry for you, and you feel it is impacting their behaviour in a negative way, you need to deal with it. It may be a simple conversation around drugs, and they are not to do them, or if you feel it has gone beyond that stage you may need to look at getting help. If they are taking drugs and you are worried, you have the right to check and search their room, and if you find some you can contact the local police, gardai and report it. It may seem really extreme to do this to your child, but they can be a good message to your child that this is not acceptable, and let the gardai, police also explain in detail the consequences of having illegal substances on them. Your child may say that all their friends are doing it and none of them have a problem blah, blah, blah. You don't care about other children; you just need to let your child know it's not ok. Get your local community garda to have a word with them, look at who they hang around with, and if some of these friendships need to be ended.

It seems really unfair to do this, but not doing it and the problem getting worse into the future will lead to even harder and tougher decisions to be made about your child and their welfare. It is your job to do the best for your child until they are an adult and you have to let your child know this. You have to put in consequences and let them know that you are not going to change your mind about them taking drugs. It doesn't matter if they are 16 or 17, you still need to parent them. I have worked with teenagers whose parents put in place strict consequences, and although their children didn't like it, those same children are now coming to me as adults and they understand why their parents did it and are grateful for it. You are also teaching your child about being a responsible parent in the future for your grandchildren. They won't hate you forever. Sit down with your partner, put a plan in place for your daughter, and set out the boundaries that will be in both of your houses so they can't get away with it with one parent and not the other.

 My 14-year-old son complains that we are embarrassing him all the time. At first, we were probably teasing him like normal families do, but soon realised he wasn't ok with it. Now it's turned into something that affects nearly every minute with him. We're finding it very difficult to have any sort of conversation with him and he has become very difficult at family/social events. Any advice on how we can deal with this situation?

A. The first thing is, it's normal for a teenager to feel embarrassed by the things their parents do and say. They are becoming self-conscious and don't want any added attention on them. They just want to blend into the background and to be left to it! It is ok to talk about this with your son and that you understand this is a normal way to feel about your parents in your teens.

Saying that, this situation seems like it's a bit more than just the normal teen embarrassment and he is struggling with family or social situations. Having to interact and to be seen as part of the family can sometimes be difficult for teenagers and maybe he is aware of how he is acting and doesn't feel good about that either. It might be a good idea to check in with him and see if he would like to talk about it. He may well say everything is fine and not even want to discuss it with you, but he will appreciate the fact that you asked even though he may not show it! If he has an aunt or uncle or close family friend, he may chat to them about how he is feeling or what it is he might be struggling with.

Social situations can be challenging. You can understand your son may be going through an awkward period in their teens, but there is no need for rudeness and bad manners because he is feeling self-consciousness. If this is the case, you may need to do a bit of forward planning if you have a family event or social occasion coming up and put some boundaries and consequences in place with your son. Let him know that the event is coming up, explain that you understand he doesn't particularly enjoy these things, but they are part of life and need to be done. Let him know that you are aware of how he is feeling but that this is not an excuse to be rude or disrespectful to you or other people you may meet on the day. If he breaks the boundaries or is rude, you can bring in the consequences. This may seem a bit harsh as you are setting something up and the event hasn't even taken place, but it's important for your son to know that rudeness and being disrespectful are not ok. He needs to get used to these situations, think about his behaviour, and act accordingly as he will have many events like this in his life. If he can get through the initial meet and greets and be social, you can always allow him to sulk off to a corner for half an hour to let him see that you appreciate the effort he is putting in. It's a delicate one, we've all been there, and I hope this bit of advice helps.

Q. My 13-year-old seems to be counting calories and become really conscious of her weight. She's very sporty. we're worried that she might becoming overly obsessed! Any suggestions?

A. In the past we have spoken about the importance of nutrition and your children, and as parents, trying to give them as balanced a diet as possible. One of the things I've seen over the years is teenage girls, in particular, taking control of their food intake and dropping out of team sports, and therefor trying to control their weight through their food. It's trying to get the balance right. It's great that she is aware of the foods that are good and bad for her health, but make sure this is not getting out of control and possibly leading to the first steps of an eating disorder.

If you are really worried, if your daughter is losing weight, dropping out of activities, or becoming increasingly withdrawn and lethargic, go to your local doctor as soon as possible to get their advice and have your daughter checked over. If you think it is the start of something and you feel you can open up a conversation with your daughter about nutrition and health, our resident nutritionist, FooDee, has courses for families around nutrition. This could help to bring up the topic and get the best advice for everyone in terms of what our bodies need daily to keep us fit and healthy. It will be advice coming from a different person, so your child may take more notice of it as it's not coming from the parents and feels like another thing they have to do. It's good to know the importance of all the different food groups and how much we need to run our bodies every day.

Some teenagers feel that if they become vegetarian and cut out meats and some carbohydrates they can control their weight, but ultimately they are not getting the correct nutrients from one or two food groups and if they decide to be vegetarian then they need to make sure they are eating all the appropriate foods to get the daily nutrients they need especially if they are sporty.

You may need to look at what your daughter is looking at online, images of girls, people she admires, and see are their body types, lifestyles, affecting the way your daughter views herself. Are her friends having an influence on how she is behaving? At this age it's not uncommon for teenage girls to all be into the same food fad. Perhaps you could chat to some of the other parents if you know them well enough and see if their daughter is going through the same thing.

If your daughter is sporty and she is controlling her food, she is going to be hungry all the time as her metabolism will be quite fast. She may be tired and lethargic all day and wanting to sleep as much as possible. If you feel this is the case and you are worried, you may need to be a bit more confrontational with her and try to get her to explain why she is eating this way so that you can try to understand what she is going through, experiencing. If she would like to become vegetarian, get on board with it. Let her know that you are ok with that but that she needs to find good healthy recipes that will keep her full and healthy. You may not all become vegetarian but let her know that you will all eat one or two veggie meals a week, it will only do you good in the long run. You can search up recipes, go shopping for the ingredients together, and she can start cooking the meals. It can become a positive aspect of her life and hopefully will help deter her from taking extreme measures to control her weight.

If you are already worried about how she is eating, her appearance, or lack of energy, then seek medical advice.

Q. My daughter is finishing her leaving certificate this week and wants to go on holidays with her friends. My wife and I are not really comfortable with this but know she needs some down time after the stress of the exams. She's worked really hard. What should we do?

A. Leaving Certificate is a state exam in Ireland, the results of which will determine where you go to college. It is an extremely stressful time for school-leavers, with parents, students, teachers, applying a certain amount of pressure all at the same time. There is a lot of expectation that the results gained from these exams will set out the future for everyone, although this of course in reality is not the case, but in the moment all they can see are the results.

Nowadays, groups of school-leavers going away on their holidays after the exams is just normal. They need to relax, shake off the stress, and enjoy themselves for a week. The media, of course, will portray these holidays as booze and sex cruises and teens behaving like animals. Some of this goes on, it's to be expected, and you would be naïve to think it doesn't. There is also a lot of sleeping that goes on, and most teens come home paler then when they went!!

You need to trust your child, sit down have the conversation about over-drinking, smoking, drugs, sex, and tell them you hope they will be safe. Your child needs to be allowed to grow up, experience this holiday. You will deal with whatever comes up if it does. They will learn so much too, and maybe they will come home and tell you that you were right!!

This is a big step for her, she will learn so much about herself and her relationship with you will be better for it too. If she comes back the worse for wear, don't tell her you told her so, she'll know and won't need you to rub it in her face. Let her go!

Q. Our son turned 13 a few months ago and it's like someone flipped a switch to turn on adolescent moodiness. He has always been a pretty good-natured kid, so this is a noticeable change in his personality. He's also had an amazing growth spurt the last 6 months and his energy level seems to be affected.

His dad & I laugh about it amongst ourselves, but I do

wonder if we should be concerned. Are there some signs we should be on the lookout for that this is something beyond typical teenage hormonal stuff?

A. Straight away what this seems like is normal teenage behaviour. Teenagers of this age become more moody and lethargic. Hormones have really started to kick in, and at first, it's very difficult for children of this age to understand what is going on and to control these emotions. Your son will feel that he is not a child anymore, that he is moving more towards being an adult and should be treated in a different manner. Unfortunately, his brain has not developed at the same rate as his appearance and he will still have child-like behaviour and thoughts until he learns to grow and mature into an adult.

I wouldn't worry too much about his behaviour. The lethargy comes with the teenage years and they need a lot more sleep than we think or that they give themselves. Like when they were young babies, they are going through another big developmental stage physically and mentally and sleep and rest are needed. If his school is noticing him falling asleep in class then you will need to look at his nighttime routine, what time he is going to bed and when is he falling asleep? Does he have a computer, phone, or tv in his room that may be causing him to stay awake longer at night? This will have a knock-on effect on his sleep and will make the waking hours so much more difficult for your son. Your son may not be aware of how much he needs a proper sleep routine. If this is the case for your son, look at introducing a cut-off time for use of devices, turn the Wi-Fi off at night, and make sure that he isn't taking anything into the room that may cause him to go to sleep later. This may seem extreme, but we as adults do it too and are very aware of the impact that having our mobile phone in use before sleep can affect our night's sleep.

This will be an ongoing issue with your son for the next few years as he goes through the teenage process, but if you get a good routine in place now in terms of sleep, rest, nutrition, and use of devices, it will be a great advantage to your son in the future. It's about routine and consequences and being there for your son too.

Q. My son and his friends have been planning a big night out after getting their leaving certificate results today. I'm not comfortable with this as I've heard so many stories about kids getting drunk and horrible things happening to them. I know I can't stop him going out but have you any advice on how I tell him to take it easy and be careful?

A. There is your starting conversation. Tell him to "take it easy and be careful and know that if you need me call me. I probably won't sleep tonight because I'm going to be worried until you come in the door and know that you are safe so if you need help call me straight away but not for a lift home, get a taxi!" You can say all of this to him and he is going to let you know that he is going to be responsible, take care of himself and not drink too much if anything at all, and then you may well be helping him clean up his vomit the next morning after having forgotten all the sage advice you gave him!!

We have to let our children just go and experience life sometimes, blow off steam and be a bit stupid. We can only give them advice and hope that they will hear it and think about their actions when they are out. Don't go overboard as he will most likely tune out and not hear anything you are saying. Just let him go, try to relax and deal with the aftermath if it happens in the following days. Your son has been under a lot of pressure after studying for exams, and then sitting them, and he will need to find a release for this. Hopefully he won't go too mental and will have a great night. You will need to try and not worry too much as this worrying won't serve any purpose except a sleepless night for you. Whatever happens, will happen. You have advised him the best you can and hopefully he'll have a great night. If you want him home at a certain time, suggest picking him up. The worse thing that happens to most teenagers on a night out is a very sore head for a couple of days after.

Q.

My 14-year-old son won't get out of bed and says he doesn't want to go to school. I'm really worried as he is in 3rd year in secondary and about to do his state exams. What can I do to get him moving?

A.

It's really hard for parents of children this age. I will always say that age 14 is the most difficult age for children and their parents. They are no longer children but not yet adults and haven't fully developed their maturity. There is a good reason why alcohol is not available to people under the age of 18, or 21 in America, as our brains have not fully developed.

A 14-year-old has not got the maturity to fully understand the world, but sometimes are physically big enough, and feel they can make the decision about whether or not to go to school.

Firstly, if your child is refusing to go to school, what are they doing that is keeping them in bed? Do they have access to a mobile phone, laptop, or game console in their room? All of these luxuries should be confiscated from your child so as to make it as uncomfortable and boring for them as possible to be in the house.

If they are going to stay around the house or in bed all day without their devices, make them get up and give them a number of jobs to do. You need to keep on at them and make them aware that you are around and are going to make it as difficult as possible for them to enjoy themselves.

Sometimes we may need additional supports to help get our child out of bed and into school. It is perfectly acceptable to get in touch with their school and get some advice on how to deal with the situation.

If it is a major problem, you could contact the local community guard and get them to have a chat with your child regarding the implications of them not attending school. There is also the local education welfare officer who may be able to give advice. You can explain to them that you are struggling to get your child to school.

Be sure to get rid of the comforts from their room. You could, if need be, threaten to drench them with a bucket of water if they don't get up. I have used this tactic in the past on a couple of children I was with on a residential trip away. They were given a warning, refused to get up and then had a bucket of cold water thrown over them. They got up, no one likes sleeping in a cold, wet bed!

You need to look at what your child is contributing to the house. Do you need to be giving them more responsibilities and making them more accountable in the home? They need to know that they cannot lie around the house all day and refuse to go to school.

Q. My son is smoking weed in his bedroom every night. He stays up until all hours and just doesn't listen to us at all. He's stopped taking part in his sports and definitely doesn't study at all. He is starting his state exams this week. We're at an absolute loss as to what to do.

A. This is a regular worry for many parents of teenage children. Smoking weed has become more common amongst teenagers and for some, not all, it's a daily occurrence. Some will try it and grow out of it, but you need to be on top of this. You need to put in place action now that will hopefully cease your son's smoking so that it doesn't become an addiction and possibly a worse drug habit in the future. You also need to see if this is impacting on other members of your family. Do you have other children in the house, is his behaviour disruptive to them? Can you smell weed in the house, never mind the legal implications of having the drug in your house. What if he falls asleep smoking a joint, probably unlikely, but not impossible?

Putting aside the dropping out of sport for now, let's deal with the smoking weed. You will need to put consequences in place for his behaviour. You need to look at the devices he has access to in his room (i.e. phone, PlayStation, laptop, tablet). If these devices are enabling him to stay awake longer at night, interfering with his sleep, then you need to take them away. He needs to start seeing and understanding that his behaviour is not acceptable. He is a child, under your care and living in your house and you need to set the boundaries, implement the consequences to keep him safe, and ultimately help him to stop smoking weed and get his life back to a more normal routine.

If you are really struggling, you can always get in touch with your local police, Garda station and see if the community officer for the area can come in and have a chat with your son. If you need extra supports get them and use them. If they were involved in sport, is there a coach or other teammates who could talk to him? Try and building supports around him so it's not only you that's trying to deal with this situation, and he has someone else to vent to. Does he have an aunt or uncle close to him who he may be more willing to listen to?

It's never ok to smoke in your home or in his bedroom and it needs to stop. You could remove the door from his bedroom, may seem extreme but it does have a good impact as there is little privacy. Don't forget this is your home for you and your other children too, and he needs to respect this. He cannot be allowed to control everything. If you need to get outside professional help, get it. Your son will be living very much in the present and won't be thinking long term. He needs to see that if he wants to go out at the weekends with friends and needs money, he needs to think about getting a job. If he wants to get involved again in sports, then encourage him to try something he would be really interested in. He may try out a few different sports but keep him interested and be interested for him.

When it comes to the exams and you feel he hasn't been studying much and may not do well, so be it. There is nothing you can do and perhaps he needs to sit the exams and see how little he did and feel disappointed in himself so as to encourage him to do better in the future. Allow natural consequences to happen for your son, they are really difficult for parents to see happen but sometimes the biggest lessons are learned. He will feel so much worse for not doing well than you ever will and that is punishment enough sometimes.

He may see that he has made it more difficult for himself to go to third level this year and may have to repeat exams. He will need to get a job for the summer, contribute to the house, and deal with consequences if he is not participating. He will need to deal with the exam results and then decide the next step. He will soon realise that his behaviour is only delaying his chances of moving on with his life and gaining more independence from you.

Hopefully this information helps, but it is going to get time, commitment, and hard work for everyone over the next few weeks.

Q. My son is 14 and is taller than both me and my husband. He's begun to get more aggressive and is trying to intimidate us to get what he wants. What can we do to change this worrying trend?

A. That is a very scary situation for parents to deal with. I always say to parents that it is not ok to be physically aggressive with your children in order to deal with a situation, especially when they are small. Imagine what it must be like for a small child to have a large person being forceful and aggressive with them, and this is the same person they rely on day in, day out to feed them, care for them, show them love and happiness. If you are going to physically punish your child when they are younger, there is a good chance that when they are older and possibly bigger than you, they are going to do the same to deal with a situation, as their brains have not fully developed as teenagers and they can't see that what they are doing isn't right as this was the way they were disciplined when they were younger. It's really important for parents, even with younger children, not to be physically aggressive towards them as a form of punishment.

This lady is in this position that her 14-year-old son is now bigger than her and her husband. I have seen this parental situation happen between small, 5-foot grannies and their much bigger grandchildren, but the granny has complete control over the situation because there is respect. So perhaps now is the time to sit down with your son and have a conversation about respect and what is ok and what is not. I'm sure your son will sit and listen, but it will all go out the window the next time there is a confrontation in the house. This is when you need to look at the consequences that will be put in place if his behaviour continues and you need to be consistent with them. The consequences have to be strong enough that he stops to think about his behaviour and realise that it's not worth it. You may not be able to do that yourself especially if your son is exceptionally aggressive towards you and you are frightened. I have said many times before on this programme that it is ok to involve the local police if you are struggling to deal with an aggressive child. If you allow your son to treat you like this, he will think it is ok and won't stop, but if you call the police and let him know that they are coming to deal with him, he will see how serious it is and will think twice about his course of action in the future. Ring your local station, let them know what is happening and don't be afraid to make a statement against your child. They will get a caution, they won't be arrested or have a criminal record, but they will know how serious the situation is, and if they continue to do it they will be told what will happen to them in the future, which will be much more serious than just a caution.

It's a very difficult thing to do to your child, but maybe you have to if you are struggling with him. Look at the support around you, grandparents, aunts, uncles and get them to help you too. Ask them to chat to your son, they will probably be listened to more than you, and it may start to sink in if there is continued support and conversations with your son about their behaviour. If there is a youth worker or teacher that your son is close to, they may be able to have a chat with him too.

TODDLERS

Q. How do you get a 2-year-old to sleep? He is my 5th child and I can't remember how I dealt with it before. He hasn't slept much over the last couple of months.

A. Sleeping is a very common issue for parents. A couple of practical things to look at could be their sleep routine during the day and the bedtime routine in the evenings. Are they napping during the day, and if so, for how long? If they are having a nap of over an hour at this age it might be worth looking at reducing this by even 10 or 15 minutes. Some parents will argue that their child becomes cranky later in the day and needs the nap, but this nap will eventually have to go as the child progresses to Montessori and then primary school. Reducing the nap time a little during the day will mean your child will be awake more and may have the desired effect on the night time sleep.

How active is your child during the day? With the introduction of tablets to children as young as your child's age, it is possible they may be less active then they should be. Have a look at the activities your child is doing during the day. At 2, most children are very busy and want to be up and about all day. Life can be very busy, and sometimes you need 10 or 15 minutes from entertaining your child to do something in the house, and that's normal, but check if they are inactive during the day and try to keep them busy. There are always little jobs they could be involved with.

If there isn't one already, perhaps look at introducing a bedtime routine, which should start about an hour before your child goes to bed. This should be a time of winding down and getting your child into a calm state of mind. Many children will watch TV at this time and that's fine, but perhaps take a closer look at the type of TV they are watching. If the cartoon or programme is very busy, loud, or full of fast action, this will have the opposite effect that you are trying to create for your child at this time. I would also advocate not allowing a TV or tablet in your child's room as it greatly effects their sleep.

If you are struggling with getting your child involved in the bedtime routine, perhaps introduce a star/reward chart for the different parts of the routine (i.e. putting on pyjamas, brushing teeth). Some people may feel 2 is too young, but if you approach it in a light-hearted, fun way, it will encourage them to get into the habit of the routine and show them how much it helps you when they are helpful too.

Q. How can I stop my 3-year-old from pretending she is a dog?

A. Don't stop her, let her do it. How many adults to you know that go around pretending to be a dog? None! Leave her to it, even join in with her and have some fun. The chances are she will get bored of looking at you pretending to be a dog. Just enjoy it with her. Make light of it and don't draw to much attention to the behaviour, she will grow out of it.

Q. Our daughter has just turned 3 and we are putting her in day care. How do we make this transition easier for her? Until now, she was with her grandmas during the day. I hate to think she will suffer, and I had a really terrible time at day care as a kid and I don't want her to have the same terrible experience I did. Any guidance?

A. This is a situation that all parents face when they decide to put their children in childcare and trust someone outside of the family will take care of them as well as you. It is even more worrying when you have had a bad experience yourself and it's difficult to detach those feelings. You will need to firstly make right with yourself the fact that the experiences your child will have in childcare will not be like your own, and that this will be a very positive step for them in their new little world.

I recently gave a talk to parents in a school and the conversation came around to their own experiences of pre-school and school. Some had really negative experiences, while others had very positive memories of this time. The biggest thing to remember is that whatever this time was like for you growing up, what your child experiences could be completely different. Your child could walk in on the first day and end up having the time of their lives and you get the opportunity enjoy this time as a parent. The first day will, of course, be worrying and possibly upsetting for all, maybe even a few tears, but that's normal. You have decided to leave your child in the care of professional people, and you need to trust them and the work they do. They will be well used to seeing first time droppers and the emotions involved, and they may well tell you to just leave your child even if she is upset because they are used to the process, and usually a parent hanging around for longer than necessary can just fuel the upset in the child. They know that within a few minutes your child will be distracted and happily participating with the class.

Childcare is run very differently now, it is a lot more child-focused and the behaviour of the carers is closely monitored, and they have strict standards to uphold. If your child does initially tell you they don't want to go, it's the first easy step in building resilience in your child and making them aware that somethings just need to be done for their own good and development, although this may be difficult to explain to your 3-year-old daughter. I'm sure you know other people who haven't had great school experiences, but they are ok and leading normal everyday lives.

Enjoy the moment, shed the tears, and look forward to all her news when she comes home. If you feel she's not settling, the staff will get in touch with you, or vice versa, and you can meet and discuss what's going on.

Q. My nearly 3-year-old is successfully potty trained and is now exceptionally proud of his poo and wants to show everyone in play school and anyone who comes into the house. What do I do?

A. Have a parade, get bells and whistles and let him show off. For a child who is 3 or 4 learning to potty train is a really big deal. We make a big deal of it every time they manage to use the toilet themselves successfully, so why can't he do it for himself? It will run its course and he'll move onto the next big life step. As long as no one is getting disgusted by it, then just leave him and his poo be!

Q. My 5-year-old has a lot of difficultly around having water on their face. It makes fun activities like swimming or general showers really difficult as he can get really upset. Any suggestions?

A. I remember our daughter having difficulty with water on her face especially when trying to wash her hair—you would think she was being murdered! Of course, as your child gets older, this can be an issue especially when you want to get them involved in swimming or water activities.

There are a few things you can try. This may take a bit of time, so patience and consistency will be needed over the next few weeks for this to work. Slowly start to introduce water onto your child's face. There are caps that you can put on your child when you are washing their hair that allows the water to run off your child's head but not directly onto their face. You could give them a dry face cloth they can hold to their eyes; it won't stop their face from getting wet, but at least your child can wipe their face and take away some of the water. Encourage them to wash their own face with water, it will be in their control. Introduce fun games in the bath like making bubbles in the water with their mouth or buy them a pair of goggles to wear in the bath and get some fun bath stickers to put on the bottom of the bath then during it they can start to put their face in the water and try and tell you what stickers are in the bath.

Don't push them, you don't want your child getting anxious before they even get close to the water. Take them to the pool and play the fun games with them, keep it a happy time and not one for giving out to them or getting frustrated with them. They will learn to do it; it just needs patience and loads of encouragement and love from mum and dad.

Q. My young toddler won't eat any vegetables at all. This is really concerning me and my wife. We've tried lots of different ways, but she doesn't seem interested at all. Any advice?

A. Getting this question made me think back to a time when our first-born daughter wouldn't drink water. We couldn't get her to take any at all, and I honestly thought she was never going to drink the stuff, but sure enough, as time went on, this changed, and she now drinks gallons of the stuff!

Try and look at how you are introducing the foods to your child and how long are you sticking at it. It can take 21 days for something new to be liked or not liked in the diet of a child, and it may need to be introduced in many different forms before you find the one that they like. Saying that, if there isn't a variety to your child's diet, they will become very bored very quickly with the same food. Perhaps also look at different ways to cook the vegetables, perhaps mashed is favoured over whole, and boiled, or perhaps vice versa. Disguise vegetables in sauces, a good pasta sauce can have every type of vegetable in it and if blended your child will have no idea and it's great over a type of pasta that they like.

Also check in with yourself and how you are feeling when you are trying to get your child to eat the vegetables. Small children pick up on tension very quickly and will become unsettled themselves. If your toddler is old enough to feed themselves, well most of it, leave them to it. Let them explore the vegetables themselves without hovering over them. Make sure the foods are soft enough and of bite size so your child can manage them safely.

Don't worry if your child doesn't eat them first time; try again the next evening with something different. There is a good chance that they will eventually find something they like and will stick to it. They may also go to creche or someone else's house and eat all their vegetables. There is just no telling when or where it will happen. If you are providing good healthy meals for your child, then their diet is sufficient enough with the nutrients they need. Don't make too much of this or the long-term goal of getting them to eat some vegetables will be very difficult for you.

There are those who may go on about children have 5 a day, but the stress of trying to get even the best of eaters to eat this amount of fruit or veg is difficult. The stress that you will be experiencing and perhaps passing on to your child while trying to get them to eat the vegetables will completely wipe out any good these foods will do for your body.

Our children's taste buds change and grow over the years and we become more adventurous with what we eat, so give it a bit of time and don't sweat it, you may be very surprised at what they are eating in a couple of years' time.

TWEENS

Q. A lot of my 8-year-old daughter's friends got smartphones for Christmas. I don't think this is right, as they are very young, but I don't want my daughter to feel left out and not part of the group. I'm really confused about what to do.

A. First thing I always ask a parent is where will your child be that there won't be a responsible adult around them that you trust. Most of the time your child will always be around an adult who can make contact with you if needed.

The second question you need to ask is what do they need a phone for?

If my child goes off for the day playing with her friends, does she need a phone? We didn't growing up, we went out and played with our friends without any contact from our parents and then went home at dinner time.

If you feel it's not right for your 8-year-old to have a phone, then don't do it. She may cry and put you under pressure because all her friends have one. In all honesty it's not the phone they want, it's the internet access they want. It is a minicomputer you are giving them. You can put on parental controls, but it doesn't mean their friends won't send them something you don't want them to see or stop them from seeing or reading content that they are too young to process.

We, as humans, don't reach full brain development until we are 21 years old. There are days when I turn off the news because I don't want to hear all the bad news, I can't process it. Now think of your 8-year-old daughter and how can she process news of children dying. It's too much. They find it difficult. When we were young, the news was on 2 times a day, and we never watched it. Now through social media, children are aware of what is happening globally all the time and they are becoming more anxious (i.e. terrorist bombings, kidnapping).

When we give our child a phone, we are opening their world to issues they are not yet ready to deal with. If you are going to give them a phone you need to have a chat about what they will see online, is it real or not. Most things sent between friends of your daughter's age are innocent enough, but what if they see or receive something from someone they don't know, and the content is more serious?

If you decide to give them a phone, talking about being safe online and social media safety is just as important a conversation as stranger danger, sex, drugs. There is also monitoring software available for parents which can be a great benefit when starting out with phones. Have the conversation with your child and let them know that you will be monitoring their phone.

It is also important to keep in mind that the age of consent for access to most social media apps is 13 years old. If your child is under this age and has access to social media apps with an age consent, one of two things may have happened. Firstly, they may have signed up to the app without your consent or knowledge, or secondly, the parent may have signed up for them. The age limit is set for a reason, for your child's safety, and being of an appropriate age when they can deal with certain issues better.

You will need to continue to have conversation with your child about online safety as they get older. You will at some point need to have a conversation with your child about pornography. Most children of teenage years with a phone will have seen pornography of some description. You need to have a discussion with your son or daughter that what they may see is not how a normal sexual relationship in a loving relationship is. This is not the expectation from a girl or boy or what they need to live up to when it comes to having sex.

Continued monitoring and conversations with your child are needed to keep them safe online whenever you choose to give them their first phone.

Q. Our 9-year-old daughter is starting to be invited to sleepovers in her friends' houses. While we don't have major issues with this, we do have some concerns about the level of supervision that goes on with some of the other parents, like watching unsuitable movies or unsupervised access to the internet. We don't want to see her miss out on these fun things, but how can we keep her from seeing things we don't want her to see without getting into a disagreement with her friends' parents?

A. This is a very tough situation to be in and it's not uncommon, so how do you have the conversation? I'm sure you have heard from your child how their friend has a phone and is allowed on social media, or there are no restrictions in place on the content they watch. This is something you don't want for your 9-year-old and that's good parenting. All you can do is concern yourself with your child, so if you don't think something is right for your child like movies for an older age group, or unrestricted access to social media that has age restrictions, you have the right to step in and explain this to your daughter's friend's parents. You can have the conversation with your daughter about the rules that are in your house in terms of the movies she is allowed watch, or the apps you have allowed to access in your house under your supervision. You can explain that you would like your child to follow these rules when they are in their friend's house too.

You can let your daughter know that you will have a chat with her friend's parents around the phone, internet access you are allowed to have. You want to have contact with the parents to chat over the details of the sleepover anyway. You can have the chat with them about the phone/internet use and that you don't allow your child unrestricted use. You are not saying that they do, but you are just discussing with them what your daughter is allowed and not allowed to do. Just check with them that this is ok. If the parents seem to have no problem with their children watching over-age movies or unlimited internet access, you can say to them that it's not ok for your child or us, so maybe we will hold off on the sleepover for now. Your child will be upset and disappointed, that's normal, but the bigger issue is your child's safety and allowing them to grow up according to their age and not see things that they are not mentally able to deal with. You don't have to be aggressive about it with the parents, but you need to stick to your principles about this.

Q. My son is 11, and right now his growing and hunger are the main issue. I can't keep this kid full. It's affecting schoolwork. Any suggestions? He always eats a good wholesome breakfast (eggs/cereal) and is packed good snacks (fruits/grains/meats). Any ideas on what else to do?

A. I have my own ideas on this, but I wanted to get some professional advice, so I got in touch with our nutritionist specialist, FooDee. She advised to keep an eye on the 4 main food groups, protein, fats, carbs and vitamins and minerals. Denise was suggesting that perhaps the breakfast of eggs and cereal is not enough. The eggs are great, but he may need to include a tomato and some cheese too. Breakfast cereal is mainly just carbohydrates, so your son will need some fats and proteins too, so he feels fuller for longer. The same needs to be done with the snacks your son is eating so there is a mix of all the food groups to sustain him during the day. You don't want to be giving him loads of fats every day, it will need to be mixed up, and try and stick as healthy as possible. Hopefully this will help your son to keep a higher level of energy and he won't be feeling sluggish in school or when he gets home in the evening. This inclusion of all of the food groups can continue into dinner and then perhaps a cereal before bed so he's not waking up hungry and trying to start the day on the back foot. Cereals have their place in our diets, but they don't necessarily fuel us all morning. Some yoghurt, or cheese, or a slice of toast with peanut butter will help even more in the mornings.

Q. With all the talk in the news about consent, how do I talk to my daughter about what is consent and how to know what's right for her?

A. With the press coverage now in relation to a rape trial in Northern Ireland, the discussion around consent is being widely reported and discussed. Sometimes parents are afraid to bring up the issues of consent with their sons or daughters. Consent must apply to everyone. I've worked with both young teenage boys and girls and it was the girls who were a bit more flexible in their consent. The boys were more hesitant and careful about how they proceeded physically with a girl and said they would respect their boundaries sexually. Now they could just have said this at the time, but they seemed genuine enough. The girls were more accepting of their partners perhaps hitting them once and be forgiven but wouldn't let them do it again. Also, they were likely to get involved in certain sexually activity quicker than perhaps they were comfortable with as they felt this is what was expected of them and everyone was doing x, y or z.

There are a few different elements involved here. Easier access to pornography and our children's exposure to pornography, and the unrealistic portrayal of what a healthy sexual relationship is. The second thing is it's ok to say no at any point. It doesn't matter how a girl is dressed or how she was engaging with a boy. If at any point a girl says no while they are kissing or fondling, then the boy needs to respect this and stop. This needs to be said by parents to their sons and daughters so that both are approaching any relationship with another person respectfully. Your daughter needs to know that she can say stop at any point if she is not comfortable in a situation. You need to have this conversation with your children if you know they are at this stage, especially young teenagers. Your 9-year-olds won't necessarily need to know this yet, but there can be a general, lighter discussion about the topic. When your child goes out, make sure they have access to a mobile phone and give them a code word to use with you, so you know they are in a situation they are not comfortable with. They can text you the word or call you, and you can pick them up or arrange a taxi to get them home. It doesn't matter if your child is somewhere you didn't expect them to be, that's not the important issue at that moment. You need to get them home and safe and if they don't wish to discuss what happened when they get home that's ok too. There will be plenty of time over the following days to have the more serious discussions about where they were and what happened.

We talk to our kids in a roundabout way when they are growing up about keeping their bodies private especially when it comes to strangers or even people they know, and this is no different. It doesn't matter that they know these people or are friends with them, consent and the right to say no are very important and just as important as the conversations when they were younger about keeping their bodies private.

Q. What's the best age to start talking to your kids about sex? I have a 7-year-old and I don't want to tell her too much too early, but at the same time, I don't want to leave her learning from her friends.

A. Many parents are not quite sure when to start this conversation with their children. Children can develop at different ages, so for those who may be physically changing sooner, they may have questions at an early age, and so the conversation will need to start then. It is definitely an individual age discussion. You can always start off easy, the first question is usually how babies are made, so starting with egg and sperm making a baby which grows in mammy's belly is usually a good start without having to go into too much more detail. Maybe pick up an age appropriate book that you can go through together, just read the page you feel is relevant and let them ask questions. More than likely, they will be happy with this and won't bother you again for a few months. Schools are introducing health education classes early in primary school, which is a good healthy environment to do it in as it's just a normal part of growing up and learning. Also having these discussions in front of both boys and girls at an early age makes both sides aware of what the other is going through developmentally and physically.

Q. My 11-year-old son is really forgetful. He forgets to pack his school bag or forgets to bring things home when he's been away or doesn't remember simple jobs that he has to do around the house, and he ends up getting in trouble or we end up getting really frustrated. Have you any suggestions as to ways we can help to get him more focused?

A. This may not seem like a major issue, but it can wind you up, and it's something your son will need to improve on as he gets older and you are less likely to be doing things for him. When I run a parenting course, these smaller issues never come up as being a problem, it's always bigger issues, but a number of continuous smaller problems can lead to major frustration and fighting in the home.

Most of the time you will look over this issue, cast your eyes to above, swear under your breath and deal with it, but it's a simple request and one that your son should be doing. You want to support your child and help them as much as possible, but they need to take over the responsibility as they get older. So, start small. If your son is forgetful and you try to get him to remember too much too soon, this problem will never be resolved, and you and your son will not move on as quickly as you may like.

I'm sure there are some parents listening to this who feel that your son should be able to remember all the things you ask him to do regardless of how many that might be, but all children are different, and some just don't have the focus to remember the not-so-important things in life, like lunch or PE gear. Treat this situation as if you are dealing with a child who is somewhat younger. If you are in school time, pick a couple of things he needs to remember to do each day (i.e. lunch in bag or making sure all his books for the next day are in his bag). Do up a little check list that you go through with him the evening before so he has all his books for the next day, it will only take a matter of minutes, and if you want, you can go through it with him the first couple of times. You could do it in the morning too, but make sure you get up a little earlier so that it's not rushed or forgotten about completely as he will never get into the routine of remembering things.

If he manages to do this successfully over the next couple of weeks and remembering these items is routine, then you can move onto introducing a couple of other things to remember. This will be a slow process with ups and downs, but he will get there. He may just be a child whose head is in the clouds, part of his personality, and all you can do is help him realise that he needs to take responsibility for certain parts of his life.

If you feel he is deliberately forgetting things or not doing as asked when you have made it as simple as possible for him to remember, you may need to bring in some consequences to jolt him in to remembering what he needs to do.

Q. Hi Allen, I am 8 years old. How can I get my parents to buy me a puppy?

A. What I would do is start to talk about puppies a lot and how important it is to learn to be responsible for something else other than yourself like a pet. Let your parents know how involved you would be in looking after the puppy, like taking them for walks, cleaning up their poo, and feeding them. Start to get loads of pictures together of the kind of puppy you would like and put them up on the walls. If it's your birthday soon, or Christmas is coming, keep talking about the puppy, but remember a puppy is not just for Christmas or your birthday—it will need your love and care every day of its life. There will be loads of poos and pees on the floor to clean up, and they will cry at night for a bit, but as long as you are going to take care of them, and your parents know this, then hopefully they will see that getting you a puppy will be a good idea.

Acknowledgements

This book could not have happened without the help of a number of people. Firstly, Julie, who basically transcribed and made sense of my ramblings. Con, Mary, Colin & Helen for the ongoing support and encouragement. Without the guidance and knowledge on the writing process over the past number of years, I'd have been lost without the amazing Maria Fowler. You're an absolute star! Without Karen Devine planting the seed of a book in my head, we definitely wouldn't be here right now. To all my friends and family, thanks for putting up with me being missing in action so much. Finally to all the young people and families I have worked with over the years, without you sharing your lives and trusting me, I would never have been able to do this. Thank you all from the bottom of my heart.

Allen O'Donoghue

Allen is a professional coach, trainer and facilitator with over 20 years of experience in youth and family development. With qualifications in Transactional Analysis Psychotherapy, Social Science and Logosynthesis, Allen's specialist knowledge and understanding of family dynamics has supported hundreds of young people and adults in setting and achieving their personal goals.

This experience has brought Allen to become a highly regarded speaker on family coaching, appearing regularly on radio and presenting at international events.

Allen also runs the highly successful Business & Life Coaching company CA Coaching www.cacoaching.ie

About Help Me To Parent

 Help Me To Parent opened its doors to parents in 2007 to great success. Through constant research and development, our programmes have consistently stayed ahead of the curve in providing practical, dynamic, and ultimately easy-to-use content, that parents can put in place as soon as they get home.

With over one hundred years combined experience in providing support to individuals and families, the Help Me To Parent team have a wealth of experience to meet any needs that parents, children, or soon-to-be parents have.

Our extensive portfolio of programmes and courses are tried and tested and have received the seal of approval from the hundreds of families we have worked with over the years.

You can find us at http://helpme2parent.ie/

Printed in Poland
by Amazon Fulfillment
Poland Sp. z o.o., Wrocław

65533954R00096